PIERRE GAGNAIRE

175 Home Recipes with a Twist

Translated from the French by Helen Woodhall
Design: Delphine Delastre
Copyediting: Anne McDowall
Typesetting and layout adaptation: Thierry Renard
Proofreading: Nicole Foster
Color Separation: IGS, L'Isle-d'Espagnac
Printed in Portugal by Portuguesa

Adapted from the French, originally published as
Bande Originale: 175 Recettes, 1 Heure de Musique
© Flammarion, S.A., Paris, 2010

This English-language edition
© Flammarion, S.A., Paris, 2012

editions.flammarion.com

12 13 14   3 2 1

ISBN: 978-2-08-020112-6

Dépôt légal: 10/2012

Photography by Jacques Gavard • Food Styling by Éric Trochon

PIERRE GAGNAIRE

175 Home Recipes with a Twist

Flammarion

CONTENTS

Introduction

Antonin Carême, the celebrated "King of Chefs, and the Chef of Kings," once declared that there were two types of cuisine: home cooking and ceremonial cooking. Through the dishes presented in this book I wish to share a personal selection of everyday recipes to suit the modern family and the varying schedules of all its members. Each one features the Gagnaire "twist," naturally, but they all remain accessible, uncomplicated, and unpretentious, demonstrating the playfulness that is characteristic of my work and allowing a touch of humor to shine through every gesture.

It has never been my intention to revolutionize the culinary arts; I have always been guided in my life as a chef by the principles of pleasure, surprise, and by the intimate conviction that it is possible to have an offbeat approach to food while still paying respect to the raw ingredients.

My roots—both social and geographical—have instilled in me this respectful attitude toward ingredients. As I was not initially enthused by the actual act of cooking or by the accompanying social niceties, I have always felt very strongly the almost elemental necessity to produce inventive food.

—Pierre Gagnaire

Before getting started

Before beginning to prepare a meal, take a moment to think about the direction the meal is going to take. Don't be tempted to prepare only new dishes; make sure that you will be making at least one tried-and-tested favorite.

Cooking is about learning about produce, learning to buy at the right price and in the right season, whether at the farmer's market or in a superstore. Cooking is about love, but it is also about learning the tricks of the trade—simple but essential techniques that make all the difference.

You don't need much in the way of equipment, but what you have should be of the best quality. You don't need dozens of knives, but the ones you use should be kept razor sharp. Taste relies on the cut. It is a fundamental element in cooking. Many of my recipes involve dicing food into what is called a *brunoise* in French, that is in dice of ⅛ in. (3 mm). I also use the julienne cut—small batons 2 ½ in. (6 cm) long and ¹⁄₁₆ in. (1 mm) thick. When it comes to citrus and other fruits, I prefer a rough cut, and I adjust the size according to the recipe.

ABOUT FAT

Always use good-quality oils and butter. When heating butter, be careful not to burn it, and feel free to add more during cooking to enrich the meat or fish you are cooking.

Virgin oils should be added at the end of cooking as a form of seasoning, without heating them (which risks altering their taste). Try out different olive oils to explore their nuances—grassy, spicy, aromatic—and don't confine yourself to olive oil. Neutral oils like grapeseed or peanut oil are indispensable in the kitchen too.

WATER

I prefer to use mineral or spring water in my cooking rather than water from the faucet. Limescale may harden some vegetables during cooking, and tap water can alter their taste.

PEPPER

Pepper absolutely must be freshly ground, and never added during cooking. The aromas of freshly ground pepper are unbeatable. Ready-ground pepper simply burns the tongue and has no complexity of flavor. I use white or black peppercorns, depending on the dish—white where I want pure punch and black where I want a more rounded, aromatic, and woody taste.

ACIDITY

Acidity plays an important part in many juices and sauces, whether it is provided by a citrus fruit, vinegar, wine, or alcohol. From white meat to fruit coulis, the notes of acidity can be many and varied—from the slightly acidic to the tangy, from fresh citrussy notes to the bite of vinegar.

PRESENTATION

It's useful to have a good range of serving dishes so you can be creative in mixing and matching colors and textures to the spirit of the dish. Try serving fresh fruit salad in a wine glass, or lobster in a rustic pot. Don't try too hard, though—remember that the most important thing is the food, and the sharing of it.

Equipment

1 chopping board

2 knives

1 wooden spatula or spoon

1 flexible rubber spatula

3 non-stick skillets, varying sizes

2 large stainless steel bowls

Whisks, varying sizes

1 set of cooking pots

Fine sieve, colander

Mandoline

Plastic food wrap

Aluminum foil

Multi-use grater (for cheese, citrus fruits, etc.)

Lemon squeezer

Peppermill

Stick blender

Food processor (bowl with chopping blade, egg whisk, etc.)

Various sizes of storage containers, preferably in stainless steel or glass, in which to keep produce

Yogurts and Blends

Fresh Fruit Compotes

Spreads

Cakes and Muffins

BREAKFAST

Grains and Cereals

Eggs

Fruit

Pancakes, Waffles, Crêpes, and Co.

Grilled Sandwiches

Fruit Juices, Drinks, Infusions

YOGURTS AND BLENDS

Yogurt can be enjoyed alone, but its freshness and binding properties can also be used to good effect in many different recipes, from dressings or fruit salads to chocolate sandwiches.

PREPARATION TIME: 20 MINUTES • SERVES 4

Cream of sheep's cheese
with cucumber and green apple, maple syrup, and spiced jelly

> 2 oz. (50 g) cucumber
> 2 oz. (50 g) green apple (about ⅓ apple)
> 2 oz. (50 g) hard sheep's cheese
> 1 tablespoon *piment d'Espelette* jelly (mild pepper jelly)
> 3 tablespoons maple syrup
> 1 cup (8 oz./240 g) *caillé de brebis* (fresh cheese made from sheep's milk—
>   cottage cheese may be substituted)

Dice the cucumber, apple, and hard sheep's cheese into a brunoise (⅛-in./3-mm dice).

In a bowl, whisk together the pepper jelly and the maple syrup. Add the diced cucumber, apple, and sheep's cheese and mix well.

Whisk the fresh sheep's cheese in a large bowl until smooth and creamy. Pour into four individual bowls and top with the brunoise mixture. Serve very cold.

CHEF'S NOTE *Piment d'Espelette* is a mild pepper from the Basque region. You can often substitute paprika if *piment d'Espelette* is not available.

Fresh cream cheese with dried fruit

⅔ cup (3 ½ oz./100 g) dried figs

⅔ cup (3 ½ oz./100 g) dates

½ cup (1 ¾ oz./50 g) walnut pieces

⅓ cup (1 ¾ oz./50 g) golden raisins

2 medium pears

2 ½ tablespoons lemon juice

6 small mushrooms

1 ⅓ cups (10 oz./300 g) fresh *faisselle* cream cheese
 (cottage cheese may be substituted)

Dice the figs and dates and place in a bowl. Add the walnut pieces and golden raisins to the bowl.

Peel and core the pears, cut into pieces, and process to a purée with the lemon juice. Add this purée to the bowl containing the dried fruit and nuts and mix gently.

Peel the mushrooms using a sharp knife and remove the stems. Cut the caps into small pieces and add to the mixture of pear and dried fruits.

Turn out the fresh cream cheese into six bowls. Pour over the pear purée, and serve.

Grapefruit zest with yogurt

Zest of 2 grapefruits (removed with a potato peeler)
2 cups (1 pint/500 ml) milk
1 vanilla bean, split lengthwise
2 pinches of licorice powder
¾ cup (9 oz./250 g) lavender honey
½ tablespoon cornstarch
1 cup (9 oz./250 g) plain yogurt

First, blanch the grapefruit zest: place the zest in a large pot with cold water, bring to a boil, then remove from the heat and drain. Repeat this process one more time, and rinse the zest under cold water.

Bring the milk to a boil with the split vanilla bean and licorice powder. Add the honey and blanched grapefruit zest.

Remove the pot from the heat, cover tightly with plastic wrap and leave to cool completely.

When it is completely cooled, strain the milk to remove the grapefruit zest and vanilla bean and return it to the clean pot. Return the pot to the heat and bring the milk to a boil again. Add the cornstarch, whisking to incorporate, to thicken. The consistency should resemble thin custard.

Remove from the heat and allow to cool, stirring from time to time to avoid a skin forming. Set aside in the refrigerator.

To serve, mix equal quantities of yogurt and grapefruit milk in individual bowls.

Grapefruit pith with buttermilk

Pith of 2 grapefruits
Scant 1 cup (6 ½ oz./180 g) sugar
1 star anise
8 ½ cups (4 ¼ pints/2 liters) mineral water
½ cup (2 ¾ oz./80 g) whole pistachios
1 ⅔ cups (13 ½ fl. oz./400 ml) fermented buttermilk
1 cup (7 oz./200 g) passionfruit pulp (about 8 or 9 fruits)

Dice the grapefruit pith and blanch it: place in a pot of cold water, bring the water to a boil, then remove from the heat and drain. Repeat this process, then rinse under cold water.

Clean out the pot and place in it the sugar, star anise, mineral water, and blanched grapefruit pith and bring to a boil.

Lower the heat and simmer slowly, covered, until the pith is translucent and shiny.

Remove from the heat and allow to cool. Remove the star anise. When the mixture has cooled, stir in the pistachios.

To serve, mix buttermilk and pith to taste and top with a little passionfruit pulp.

CHEF'S NOTE Buttermilk was originally the liquid that ran from the butter churn when butter was being churned. Nowadays it is known as fermented buttermilk (it is made like yogurt but with a different bacterial culture); it usually has a fat content of between 1 and 3 percent.

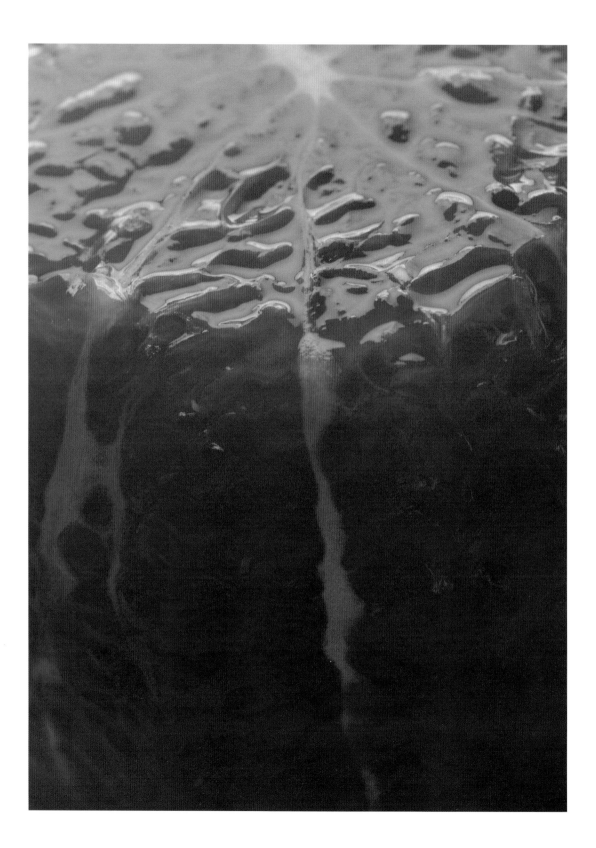

Grapefruit with raïb

1 Royal Gala apple

1 banana

⅓ cup (1 ¾ oz./50 g) dried apricots

Flesh of 2 peeled grapefruits

3 ½ tablespoons (1 ¾ oz./50 g) butter

Scant ½ cup (3 oz./85 g) brown sugar

4 ¼ cups raïb (2 pints/1 liter) (or plain yogurt)

Peel and dice the apple. Cut the banana into ¼ in. (5 mm) rounds. Dice the dried apricots. Chop the grapefruit flesh.

In a pot, melt half of the butter, add the diced apple and sweat for 2–3 minutes, then add two tablespoons of sugar. Leave to caramelize for a few minutes, then remove from the pot and set aside in a bowl.

In the same pot, melt the remaining butter and 2 tablespoons of sugar and caramelize the banana slices. Remove and add to the apple.

Place the grapefruit flesh and 2 tablespoons of sugar in the cooking pot. Cook over a high heat, stirring, until the grapefruit flesh breaks down and renders its juice, then turn down the heat and cook until the juice is reduced by half.

Return the apple and banana to the pot, mix carefully with the grapefruit, then remove the mixture from the pot and allow to cool before adding the diced apricots.

To serve, mix a spoonful of the grapefruit marmalade with raïb or yogurt to taste.

CHEF'S NOTE Raïb is a fermented milk product, similar to the North African lben.

FRESH FRUIT COMPOTES

These fruit compotes are sweetened with a spiced syrup.

PREPARATION TIME: 5 MINUTES · MACERATION TIME: 1 WEEK · MAKES ABOUT 3 ¼ CUPS (750 ML)

Spiced syrup

1 25-fl. oz. (750-ml) bottle of cane sugar syrup
1 stick cinnamon
2 slices fresh ginger root
1 strip of lemon peel
4 kaffir lime leaves

Simply add all the flavorings to the bottle of cane sugar syrup and seal. Allow to infuse for a week in a cool dark place. Once reopened, keep in the refrigerator.

CHEF'S NOTE The kaffir lime (or combava) has a very aromatic leaf. Its aroma can be pervasive if overused, so err on the side of caution if you are not used to this ingredient.

Apricot, white peach,
and melon compote

1 small Cavaillon melon

2 fresh apricots (Bergeron variety if available)

1 white peach

2 tablespoons golden raisins

Scant 1 cup (7 fl. oz./200 ml) Spiced syrup (see page 22)

2 tablespoons orange marmalade

Cut the melon in half, peel, remove the seeds, and cut the flesh into cubes. Place in a bowl and set aside in the refrigerator.

Cut the fresh apricots into chunks. Peel the peach and chop roughly. Place the apricot and peach pieces in a pot with the raisins and syrup. Cook over a low heat for 10 minutes until the fruit has softened but is still a little firm. Allow to cool then place in the refrigerator.

To serve, carefully mix a little of the fruit compote with the orange marmalade and the melon cubes.

PREPARATION TIME: 10 MINUTES • COOKING TIME: 5 MINUTES
REFRIGERATION TIME: 20 MINUTES • SERVES 4

Orange, grape, and pear salad

3 oranges

2 oz. (60 g) Muscat grapes

2 pears

3 tablespoons Spiced syrup (see page 22)

3 tablespoons red currant jelly

Orange juice (optional)

Peel the oranges, removing all the pith, and cut the flesh into rough chunks, keeping the juice. Cut the grapes in half. Peel the pears and cut them into chunks.

Bring the spiced syrup to a boil, add the pear pieces, and cook for 4 minutes. Allow to cool.

In a bowl, carefully mix together the orange pieces, grapes, red currant jelly, and pear compote. Add a little orange juice if the mixture seems too thick.

Chill for 20 minutes before serving.

Fresh raspberries
with rhubarb and strawberry compote

9 oz. (250 g) rhubarb

2 tablespoons mineral water

5 tablespoons Spiced syrup (see page 22)

3 tablespoons strawberry jam

1 lb. (500 g) fresh raspberries

Peel the rhubarb and chop it into ½ in. (1 cm) slices. Place it in a pot with the mineral water. Cover and cook over a gentle heat for 3 minutes, then remove the lid and cook for an additional 2 minutes to reduce the liquid. Remove from the pot and leave in a bowl to cool.

Mix the rhubarb with the spiced syrup, then add the strawberry jam. Gently add the raspberries, and serve well chilled.

Apple and beet compote
with grated walnut

2 Royal Gala apples
3 tablespoons mineral water
Juice of ½ lemon
1 small beet (raw)
3 tablespoons strawberry jam
Scant ½ cup (3 ½ fl. oz./100 ml) Spiced syrup (see page 22)
2–3 tablespoons walnut halves (fresh if possible)

Peel the apples and chop them roughly. Place them in a pot with the water and a squeeze of lemon juice. Cover and cook over a low heat for 8 minutes, then remove and place in a bowl. Allow to cool.

Grate the beet over the warm apples, add the strawberry jam, and mix carefully. Add the spiced syrup to loosen the mixture a little.

Just before serving, grate over the walnuts and serve well chilled.

CHEF'S NOTE Gala apples tend to be small, and reddish-orange in color with vertical markings. Despite their fine skin, they are not easily bruised. They are very sweet, faintly acidic with a hint of bitterness, firm, juicy, and crunchy. There are many varieties of Gala, including ones with redder skins, such as the popular Royal Gala.

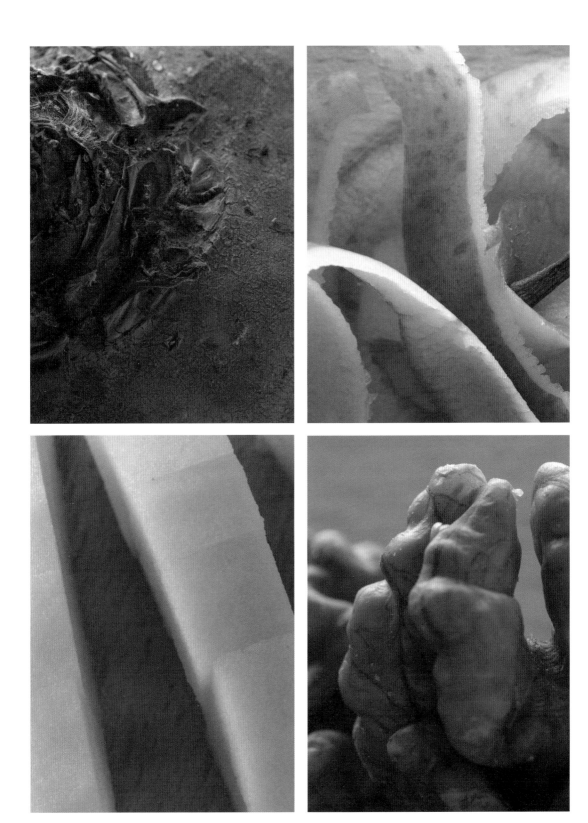

SPREADS

These spreads keep well when stored in a cool place in a covered jar.

PREPARATION TIME: 10-15 MINUTES · COOKING TIME: 10 MINUTES
MAKES ABOUT 2 ¼ CUPS (14 OZ./400 G)

Almond, evaporated milk,
and orange spread

1 ¼ cups (10 fl. oz./300 ml) orange juice
5 oz. (150 g) almond paste, crumbled
Scant 1 cup (7 fl. oz./200 ml) evaporated milk
Grated zest of 1 orange

Pour the orange juice into a cooking pot and boil until reduced by half.

Pour into the bowl of a food processor and add the pieces of almond paste, the evaporated milk, and the orange zest. Mix until you have a smooth paste.

Chocolate and hazelnut spread

1 tablespoon glucose syrup

Scant ½ cup (3 oz./80 g) sugar

1 ¾ cups (14 fl. oz./400 ml) light cream

2 tablespoons honey

4 oz. (120 g) milk chocolate (40 percent)

3 ¼ tablespoons (1 ½ oz./36 g) cocoa paste (or a chocolate with high percentage
   of cocoa solids)

7 tablespoons (3 oz./80 g) hazelnut paste

First make a caramel: put the glucose syrup and sugar in a pot and heat gently to make a light caramel.

Heat the cream and the honey together until the honey has melted, then pour into the caramel. The mixture may splash up, so be careful. Stir, and bring to a boil.

Gently melt the milk chocolate, the cocoa paste, and the hazelnut paste together, then pour the creamy caramel over this chocolate mixture. Mix well to make a smooth spread.

PREPARATION TIME: 10 MINUTES · COOKING TIME: 15-20 MINUTES
MAKES ABOUT 2 ½ CUPS (1 LB./450 G)

Caramel spread with passionfruit

1 cup (½ pint/250 ml) whole milk
1 ½ cups (10 ½ oz./300 g) sugar
¼ cup (2 fl. oz./60 ml) passionfruit juice

Put the milk and sugar in a pot and heat gently, stirring constantly with a flexible spatula, until the sugar dissolves and the mixture takes on a caramel color. Add the passionfruit juice and bring back to a boil. Whisk well until perfectly smooth.

CAKES AND MUFFINS

The following recipes are made using loaf pans: about 9 ½ in. (24 cm) in length for 1 large cake and 6 in. (15 cm) in length for 4 small ones.

PREPARATION TIME: 15 MINUTES • COOKING TIME: 20-25 MINUTES, ACCORDING TO SIZE
MAKES 1 LARGE CAKE OR 4 SMALL ONES

Weekend cake

1 vanilla bean
1 ¾ cups (11 ½ oz./330 g) superfine sugar
3 sticks plus 2 tablespoons (13 oz./360 g) butter
8 eggs
Grated zest of 1 organic lemon
3 ⅓ cups (11 ½ oz./330 g) all-purpose flour
Butter and flour for the loaf pan(s)

For the frosting:
9 oz. (250 g) fondant icing
1 ½ tablespoons (¾ fl. oz./20 ml) sugar cane syrup
1 tablespoon Kirsch

Grease and flour the loaf pan(s). Preheat the oven to 350°F/180°C/gas mark 4.

Scrape the vanilla seeds into the sugar and keep the bean for another use.

Melt the butter.

Break the eggs into the bowl of a food mixer, add the sugar and lemon zest and mix for 10 minutes. Add the flour, then the hot melted butter, and mix on a high speed for 1 minute until the mixture deflates.

Fill the loaf pan(s) to three-quarters full and bake in the oven for 20–25 minutes, according to the size and number of cakes.

Meanwhile, make the frosting. Melt all the ingredients together gently at a temperature of 130°F (55°C), without boiling. Stir to make a smooth paste. Allow to cool.

Remove the cake(s) from the oven, allow to rest for 3 minutes, then turn out onto a wire tray.

Allow to cool completely, then top with the frosting. Keep the iced cake(s) at room temperature.

Almond and dark chocolate cake

11 oz. (300 g) almond paste (50 percent)

1 egg plus 6 egg yolks

3 tablespoons (1 oz./25 g) cornstarch

¼ cup (1 oz./25 g) all-purpose flour

⅓ cup (1 ¼ oz./35 g) cocoa powder

¾ stick (3 oz./90 g) butter, melted

1 cup (7 oz./200 g) frozen raspberries

2 ½ tablespoons chocolate chips

Butter and flour for the loaf pan(s)

Grease and flour the loaf pan(s).

Preheat the oven to 350°F/180°C/gas mark 4.

In a food processor, mix the almond paste with the whole egg until smooth and pale. Add the egg yolks one at a time.

Sift together the cornstarch, flour, and cocoa powder, then add to the egg and almond mixture and mix to combine.

Pour in the melted butter, little by little, and mix again to make a smooth cake batter.

Pour a third of the mixture into the prepared loaf pan(s), scatter over the frozen raspberries, then dollop on a second layer of cake batter. Scatter the chocolate chips over, then finish with a final layer of cake batter.

Bake in the oven for 30–40 minutes until risen and firm to the touch.

CHEF'S NOTE Confectioners' almond paste is made from almonds and sugar. It can be used to cover cakes and make decorations. The percentage of almonds it contains may vary from 20 percent, for an easy-to-work paste used for decorating, up to 50 percent for a paste used as an ingredient.

Caribbean cake

4 eggs

9 oz. (250 g) almond paste (50 percent)

½ cup (1 ¾ oz./50 g) all-purpose flour

1 tablespoon (⅓ oz./10 g) cornstarch or potato starch

3 tablespoons (1 ½ oz./40 g) butter

Scant 1 cup (7 fl. oz./200 ml) Spiced syrup (see page 22)

Scant 1 cup (7 fl. oz./200 ml) Caribbean rum

Butter and flour for the loaf pan

Grease and flour the loaf pan.

Preheat the oven to 350°F/180°C/gas mark 4.

In the bowl of a food processor, mix the eggs one by one into the almond paste. Mix for 20 minutes.

Sift the flour and the cornstarch together into a separate bowl. Melt the butter.

Gently mix the flour and cornstarch mixture into the almond paste mixture, then add the hot melted butter. Combine with a flexible spatula.

Pour into the prepared loaf pan and place in the oven. Immediately turn down the heat to 325°F/160°C/gas mark 3 and bake for 18–20 minutes until risen and firm to the touch.

Combine the syrup and the rum and pour over the cake while it is still warm.

Lemon chiffon cake

Zest and juice of 1 organic lemon

1 ⅓ cups (9 oz./250 g) superfine sugar

1 sachet (2 teaspoons) vanilla sugar

6 eggs

2 ½ cups (9 oz./250 g) all-purpose flour

Butter to grease the loaf pan

Heat the oven to 350°F/180°C/gas mark 4. Butter a loaf pan. Add the lemon zest to the sugar in the bowl of a food processor. Stir together, and add the vanilla sugar and the eggs. Mix for 10 minutes until the mixture becomes pale and has doubled in volume. Incorporate the lemon juice, then the sifted flour. Pour into the buttered loaf pan and bake in the oven for 40 minutes. Remove from the oven and allow to cool on a wire tray. Serve with Lemon and rhubarb marmalade (see below).

CHEF'S NOTE It is very important to grate the lemon zest into the sugar—the sugar will "capture" the flavor of the zest and the mixture will be more highly flavored. It is best to choose organic lemons to avoid ingesting the pesticides and wax that are found on non-organic ones.

Lemon and rhubarb marmalade

2 lemons

2 cups (1 pint/500 ml) water

1 ¼ cups (8 oz./225 g) superfine sugar

9 oz. (250 g) rhubarb, chopped

Chop the lemons into pieces, place them in a cooking pot, and cover with 1 cup of water. Bring to a boil, then drain and return to the pot with the sugar and remaining water. Bring to a boil, then turn down the heat and allow to simmer for 40 minutes over a gentle heat. Add the chopped rhubarb to the lemons and cook for an additional 10 minutes until syrupy and reduced. Allow to cool to room temperature.

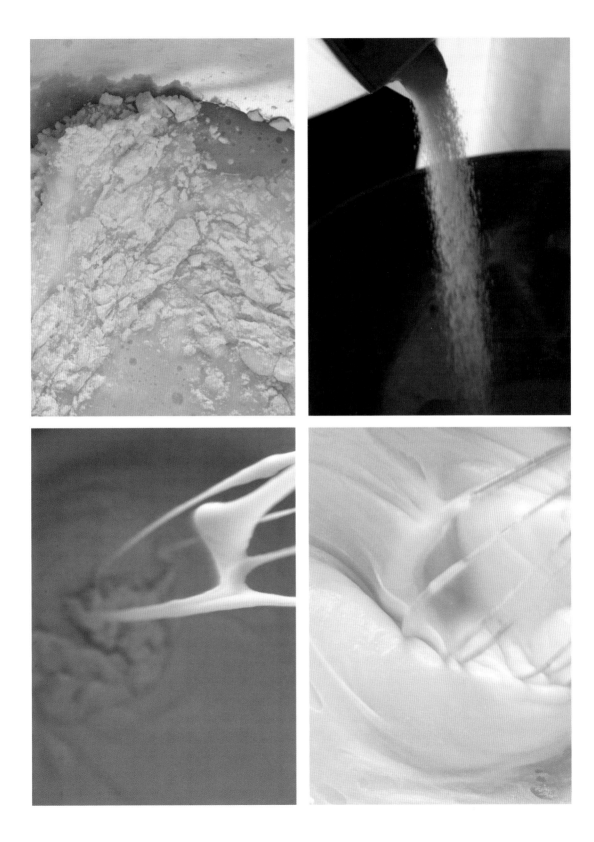

Lemon cake

1 ½ cups (5 ½ oz./160 g) all-purpose flour

Pinch of baking powder

6 egg yolks

1 cup (7 ½ oz./210 g) superfine sugar

Grated zest of 1 organic lemon

Scant ½ cup (3 ½ fl. oz./100 ml) crème fraîche
   (or sour cream)

½ cup (2 oz./60 g) candied lemon, chopped

4 tablespoons (2 oz./60 g) butter, melted

Butter and flour for the loaf pan(s)

For the syrup:

½ cup (4 fl. oz./120 ml) water

½ cup (3 ½ oz./100 g) sugar

4 tablespoons lemon juice

Preheat the oven to 350°F/180°C/gas mark 4. Sift the flour and baking powder together into a large mixing bowl. In a separate bowl, combine the egg yolks with the sugar, lemon zest, and crème fraîche. Add the flour and the candied lemon and mix to combine. Mix in the cooled melted butter. Fill the greased and floured loaf pan to three-quarters full and bake for 25 minutes. Meanwhile, prepare the syrup: bring the water and sugar to a boil and then add the lemon juice. When the cake is cooked, remove from the oven and pour over the syrup. Allow to cool on a wire cooling rack. Serve with Custard with orange and kaffir lime (see below).

Custard with orange and kaffir lime

6 egg yolks

Scant ½ cup (3 oz./80 g) sugar

2 cups (1 pint/500 ml) milk

Grated zest of 1 organic orange

Grated zest of ¼ kaffir lime

Gently beat the egg yolks and the sugar together in a cooking pot. Pour the milk into a separate cooking pot and bring to a boil. Pour the milk over the egg yolk mixture and cook over a low heat for 5 minutes, stirring constantly with a wooden spatula. Do not allow to boil or the custard will split. Once the custard has thickened, remove from the heat and pour it into a cold bowl to stop the cooking process. Add the orange and kaffir lime zest and stir. Cover with plastic wrap and set aside in the refrigerator until ready to use.

Carrot and hazelnut muffins

1 stick plus 1 tablespoon (4 ½ oz./125 g) butter

2 ½ cups (9 oz./250 g) all-purpose flour

2 teaspoons baking powder

Generous ½ cup (120 g) brown sugar

½ teaspoon cinnamon

¼ cup (1 oz./25 g) ground hazelnuts

2 eggs

Scant 1 cup (7 oz./200 ml) whole milk

5 oz. (150 g) carrot, grated (1 large or 2 medium carrots)

6 muffin cups

Preheat the oven to 400°F/200°C/gas mark 6. Melt the butter in a small pot over a low heat.

Sift the flour and the baking powder into a bowl, and add the brown sugar, cinnamon, and ground hazelnuts.

Whisk the eggs and the milk in a large mixing bowl, then add the melted butter.

Add the dry ingredients to the egg–milk mixture in the large mixing bowl, and combine, being careful not to overmix. Mix in the grated carrot.

Fill the muffin cups to three-quarters full and bake in the oven for 20 minutes. Allow to cool on a wire tray.

Banana and chocolate muffins

¾ cup (3 ½ oz./100 g) pecans

3 ripe bananas

1 stick plus 1 tablespoon (4 ½ oz./125 g) salted butter

2 ½ cups (9 oz./250 g) all-purpose flour

2 teaspoons baking powder

⅔ cup (4 ½ oz./125 g) superfine sugar

2 eggs

Scant 1 cup (7 fl. oz./200 ml) whole milk

3 ½ oz. (100 g) dark chocolate, grated (1 cup grated)

6 muffin cups

Preheat the oven to 400°F/200°F/gas mark 6.

Chop the pecans. Peel and mash the bananas. Melt the butter over a low heat.

Sift the flour and the baking powder into a bowl and stir in the sugar.

Whisk the eggs and milk together in a large mixing bowl then add the melted butter. Add all the other ingredients and combine, being careful not to overmix.

Fill the muffin cups to three-quarters full and bake for 20 minutes. Turn out and cool on a wire tray.

GRAINS AND CEREALS

These grains and cereals should be cooked in a light vanilla-infused syrup.

MAKES ABOUT 4 ¼ CUPS (2 PINTS/1 LITER)

Vanilla syrup

4 ¼ cups (2 pints/1 liter) mineral water
½ cup (3 ½ oz./100 g) granulated sugar
½ vanilla bean

Put all the ingredients in a pot and bring to a boil. Cool and set aside until needed.

PREPARATION TIME: 15 MINUTES • COOKING TIME: 30 MINUTES • SERVES 6

Amaranth with mango,
papaya, and passionfruit

1 cup (7 oz./200 g) amaranth
1 ½ cups (¾ pint/350 ml)
   Vanilla syrup (see above)
11 oz. (300 g) yellow mango
   (about 2 large mangoes)
1 papaya

3 tablespoons honey
3 tablespoons lemon juice
½ cup (4 ¼ oz./120 g) passionfruit pulp
   (from about 4 fruits)

Cook the amaranth seeds over a low heat for 30 minutes in the vanilla syrup. Remove from the heat and allow to cool in the pot without draining. Meanwhile, cut the mango into a brunoise (⅛ in./3 mm dice) and set aside. Peel and seed the papaya and cut it into a brunoise. Place the papaya dice in a pot and cook over a low heat, stirring regularly, until it is reduced to a compote. Allow to cool then refrigerate until required. Whip together the honey, lemon juice, and passionfruit pulp. Drain the cooked, cooled amaranth seeds and mix with this dressing. Divide the amaranth between six individual bowls, top with a generous spoonful of papaya compote, and finish with the mango brunoise.

Quinoa with pineapple
and persimmon

2 egg yolks

3 tablespoons sugar

1 cup ($\frac{1}{2}$ pint/250 ml) milk

1 cup (7 oz./200 g) quinoa

2 cups (1 pint/500 ml) Vanilla syrup (see page 45)

2 $\frac{1}{2}$ tablespoons brown sugar

9 oz. (250 g) fresh pineapple, cubed

6 oz. (180 g) persimmon, diced

2 $\frac{1}{2}$ tablespoons white poppy seeds

Whisk together the egg yolks and the sugar until pale and thick. Bring the milk to a boil, then pour over the egg yolk mixture, stirring continuously. Cook over a low heat, stirring all the time with a spatula, until the mixture thickens to the consistency of custard. Remove from the heat and set aside to cool.

Cook the quinoa in the vanilla syrup for approximately 15 minutes, then remove from the heat and allow to swell.

Meanwhile, put the brown sugar and the pineapple cubes in a non-stick skillet and cook over a high heat until the pineapple is caramelized. Remove from the heat.

When cooled, combine the pineapple and the persimmon.

Mix the cooled custard with the quinoa.

Place a mound of quinoa in each of six individual dishes, and divide the fruit between them. Scatter over the poppy seeds.

Pearl barley with quince jelly,
angelica, and fresh lychees

¾ cup (5 oz./150 g) pearl barley

2 cups (1 pint/500 ml) Vanilla syrup (see page 45)

7 oz. (200 g) quince jelly

5 oz. (150 g) preserved angelica, diced

24 fresh lychees, peeled and chopped

Simmer the barley in the vanilla syrup for approximately 35 minutes.

Remove from the heat and allow to swell until completely cooled, then drain.

When cooled and drained, mix in the quince jelly, angelica pieces, and chopped lychees. Divide between six individual bowls.

Barley meal
with pomegranate seeds and dried fruits

10 ½ cups (5 ¼ pints/2.5 liters) mineral water
1 cup (5 oz./150 g) barley meal
¾ cup (4 oz./120 g) dried figs, chopped
1 cup (4 oz./120 g) dates, chopped
¼ cup (1 ½ oz./40 g) raisins
1 tablespoon orange flower water
¾ cup (4 oz./120 g) fresh pomegranate seeds
Confectioners' sugar
¾ cup (7 oz./200 g) apricot coulis

Bring the water to a boil, pour it over the barley meal, and allow to swell until completely cooled, then drain.

Combine the dried fruits with the orange flower water, then add to the cooled, drained barley meal.

Divide the mixture between four bowls, scatter over the pomegranate seeds, and dust with a little confectioners' sugar. Serve the apricot coulis in a separate dish.

Brown rice
with a citrus and tomato dressing

1 cup (7 oz./200 g) brown basmati rice

½ cup (3 ½ fl. oz./100 ml) Vanilla syrup
  (see page 45)

6 tablespoons grapefruit juice

6 tablespoons orange juice

3 tablespoons lemon juice

1 tablespoon sugar

Scant ½ cup (3 ½ fl. oz./100 ml) olive oil

1 medium tomato, chopped

Cook the rice for 20 minutes in a large pot of boiling water. When cooked, drain and place in a large bowl. Stir in the vanilla syrup, cover, and allow to rest. Combine the three citrus juices and the sugar in a high-sided bowl and whisk in the olive oil a drop at a time to make a dressing. Add the chopped tomato and turn to coat the diced tomato with the dressing. Serve the sweetened rice and the tomato dressing separately, allowing guests to mix to their taste.

Indian rice pudding (kheer)

¼ cup (1 ¾ oz./50 g) white basmati rice

4 ¼ cups (2 pints/1liter) milk

2 cardamom pods, crushed

Pinch of salt

¾ cup (5 oz./140 g) sugar

Scant 1 cup (7 fl. oz./200 ml) light cream

Bring a large pot of water to a boil and add the rice. As soon as the water comes back to a boil, remove from the heat and drain the rice. Rinse out the pot and pour in the milk. Add the crushed cardamom pods and the salt. Bring to a boil, then add the rice and allow to simmer for an hour over a low heat, until all the milk is absorbed and the rice is creamy. Toward the end of the cooking time, stir in the sugar and cream. Transfer the rice pudding into a large glass bowl, cover with plastic wrap, and allow to cool in the refrigerator.

EGGS

Caramelized omelet
with muscovado sugar

2 tablespoons (1 oz./25 g) butter

4 peach halves in syrup, drained and chopped

10 strawberries, halved

8 eggs

Pinch of salt

1 tablespoon sunflower oil

2 tablespoons dark muscovado sugar (brown sugar may be substituted)

First make a fruit marmalade: heat half the butter in a skillet and add the chopped peaches and halved strawberries. Allow to reduce for 4–5 minutes over a low heat, then remove to a bowl and set aside.

Whisk the eggs with the salt in a bowl. In a large skillet, heat the oil and the remaining butter over a low heat and pour in the beaten eggs. Cook, drawing in the edges, until the omelet is nearly cooked, then sprinkle with the sugar, flip over, and finish cooking the omelet, caramelizing the sugar at the same time.

Slide the omelet onto a warmed plate, spread over the warm fruit marmalade, and serve immediately.

CHEF'S NOTE Muscovado is a brown unrefined cane sugar, available from specialty suppliers. It is also known as Barbados sugar.

Savory flans
with langoustine salad, zucchini, and chickpeas

9 oz. (250 g) small langoustines	1 garlic clove, minced
2 cups (1 pint/500 ml) milk	⅓ cup (3 ½ oz./100 g) cooked chickpeas
2 tablespoons olive oil	*Piment d'Espelette* or hot paprika
1 zucchini, grated	Salt
3 stems cilantro, snipped	2 eggs plus 1 egg yolk, beaten
1 tablespoon snipped chives	1 tablespoon toasted sesame seeds

Shell the langoustines. Put the crushed heads and shells into a large pot with the milk and warm gently. Remove from the heat, cover, and allow to infuse.

Heat a spoonful of olive oil over a high heat and quickly sauté the langoustine tails. Be careful not to overcook.

Put the zucchini, herbs, garlic, chickpeas, and fried langoustine tails in a bowl. Season with *piment d'Espelette*, salt, and a few drops of olive oil. Cover and set aside in the refrigerator.

Preheat the oven to 325°F/160°C/gas mark 3.

Prepare a bain-marie: pour boiling water into a shallow dish lined with a sheet of newsprint. Place four small bowls or ramekins in the dish.

Strain the warm infused milk and discard the langoustine heads. Combine the warm milk with the beaten eggs. Season, then pour the mixture into the small bowls or ramekins placed in the bain-marie. Cook in the oven for 25 minutes.

When the flans are cooked, remove from the oven and allow to cool. Divide the langoustine-tail mixture over the flans, sprinkle with toasted sesame seeds, and serve immediately.

Savory shrimp flans
with ham béchamel sauce

2 cups (1 pint/500 ml) whole milk

2 eggs plus 1 egg yolk, beaten

Salt and pepper

Pinch of nutmeg

1 tablespoon (½ oz./15 g) butter

1 teaspoon curry powder

3 oz. (80 g) pink shrimp, shelled

For the béchamel sauce:

1 tablespoon (½ oz./15 g) butter

1 tablespoon flour

1 cup (½ pint/250 ml) milk

1 tablespoon Parmesan

Salt and pepper

2 slices cooked ham, diced

2 stems flat-leaf parsley, snipped

Preheat the oven to 325°F/160°C/gas mark 3.

Prepare a bain-marie: pour boiling water into a shallow dish lined with a sheet of newsprint.

Place four small bowls or ramekins in the dish.

Gently heat the milk, then pour it over the beaten eggs. Season with salt, pepper, and nutmeg.

Pour the mixture into the bowls or ramekins placed in the bain-marie. Cook in the oven for 20 minutes. They should still be very slightly wobbly.

Melt the butter over a medium heat with the curry powder until the butter bubbles and is slightly browned. Add the shrimp and cook for a few seconds. Place them on the flans.

To make the béchamel sauce, melt the butter in a pot and stir in the flour. Cook over a gentle heat for about 4 minutes, mixing with a wooden spatula. Pour in the cold milk, a few drops at a time at first, stirring all the time to make a smooth sauce. If lumps form, use a whisk to rectify. Cook for 5 minutes until the sauce has thickened.

Add the Parmesan. Season and stir in the ham and parsley.

Pour the béchamel over the flans and serve immediately.

Cream of Gorgonzola
with floating islands

Scant ½ cup (3 ½ fl. oz./100 ml) light cream
5 oz. (150 g) Gorgonzola, crumbled
4 very fresh eggs
Pinch of salt
Freshly ground nutmeg and white pepper
Toasted bread, to serve

Heat the cream in a small pot. Add the Gorgonzola, whisking to give a smooth texture.

Carefully separate the eggs, keeping the yolks intact. Put the whites in a bowl.

Divide the Gorgonzola cream between 4 shallow bowls. Place an egg yolk on each one, and keep warm, taking care that the egg does not cook.

Whisk the egg whites with a pinch of salt until firm.

Place a large spoonful of whipped egg white on top of each bowl. Grate over a little nutmeg and grind over some white pepper.

Serve immediately with toast "soldiers."

Assassin's eggs

1 ½ tablespoons (¾ oz./20g) butter

Mineral water

8 eggs

2 tablespoons sherry vinegar

2 tablespoons pomegranate seeds

¼ cup (1 oz./30 g) cooked red beet, in brunoise (⅛ in./3 mm dice)

4 tablespoons Vinegar liqueur (see page 196)

Salt and freshly ground black pepper

Toasted bread, to serve

Heat a non-stick skillet, add a lump of butter and a spoonful of mineral water.

Break the eggs one at a time into a glass: it is very important that the egg yolk remains unbroken.

Add the eggs one by one and cook over a high heat for 2 minutes.

Flip them, and sprinkle with a few drops of sherry vinegar. Slide the eggs out onto warmed plates.

Add a little more butter to the same skillet, then add the pomegranate seeds and beet and cook over a high heat for 3 minutes. Add the vinegar liqueur, then pour over the eggs.

Season, and serve immediately with toasted bread.

Scrambled eggs with smoked eel

4 oz. (100 g) smoked eel

Splash of lemon juice

8 eggs

Salt and freshly ground white pepper

1 tablespoon (½ oz./15 g) butter

2 tablespoons heavy cream

Rye bread, to serve

Cut the eel into small dice and season with a splash of lemon juice.

Beat the eggs in a bowl and season with salt and pepper.

Heat the butter in a small skillet and add the eggs. Cook, stirring continuously.

When the eggs are almost cooked through, add the cream, and mix to obtain a thick purée. Check the seasoning.

Divide the egg purée between 4 ramekins, arrange some eel on each one, and season generously with pepper. Serve with slices of rye bread.

Poached eggs with wilted sorrel
and white sauce

½ cup white vinegar

4 eggs

1 tablespoon (½ oz./15 g) butter

5 oz. (150 g) sorrel leaves

Freshly ground white pepper

¾ oz. (20 g) blue cheese, crumbled

2 crackers, roughly crumbled

For the white sauce:

⅔ cup (5 fl. oz./150 ml) mayonnaise

Scant ½ cup (3 ½ fl oz./100 ml) whipped cream

2 tablespoons evaporated milk

Splash of lemon juice

Pinch of salt

Fill a large pot with water, add the vinegar and bring to a boil. Turn down to a simmer and carefully break the eggs one by one into small glasses and slip them into the simmering water. Allow to cook for 5 minutes over a very low heat.

When the whites are cooked, use a slotted spoon to take out each egg, and transfer to a clean cloth to drain.

Heat the butter in a skillet over a low heat and cook the sorrel for 3 minutes.

To make the white sauce, mix the mayonnaise with the whipped cream, add the evaporated milk, a splash of lemon juice, and season with salt.

Divide the cooked sorrel between warmed plates and place a poached egg on each one. Pour over a little white sauce. Grind over a little white pepper, and scatter over the crumbled blue cheese and crackers.

CHEF'S NOTE The proportions that go into the white sauce are pretty important. You can keep it for a while in a glass jar in the refrigerator and use it to dress a romaine salad or to serve with cold roast meat or deli meats.

Eggs poached in maple syrup

1 tablespoon vinegar

2 eggs

1 pomelo or pink grapefruit

1 Montbéliard sausage,
  or other smoked pork sausage

2 tablespoons maple syrup

Freshly ground black pepper

1 ear of corn, uncooked

Scant ½ cup (3 ½ fl. oz./100 ml) whipped cream
  (35 percent fat content)

Pinch of cinnamon

Heat a large pot of water and add the vinegar. Poach the eggs in simmering water. Remove when done and allow to cool a little.

Peel the pomelo, and roughly chop the flesh.

Heat the broiler oven. Slice the sausage and place in a shallow ovenproof dish. Broil the sausage slices, then remove from the dish to a plate using a slotted spoon.

Add the pomelo flesh to the dish and mix to combine with the melted fat. Remove the pomelo flesh and set aside.

Place the dish on the heat and reduce the juice by half. Add the maple syrup, then return the sausage to the dish to reheat. Season generously with black pepper.

Lay the poached eggs on top of the sausage and let them warm through. Grate the corn over the top.

Serve this dish hot, with the whipped cream flavored with a pinch of cinnamon.

CHEF'S NOTE *Saucisse de Montbéliard* is a smoked pork sausage spiced with cumin, nutmeg, garlic, and white wine.

Maple syrup is classified by color. The Canadian system of classification recognizes three categories (1, 2, and 3), while the system used in Quebec uses five: extra-light, light, medium, amber, and dark). The clarity, density, and the taste of the product vary with the color; the lighter the syrup, the higher its classification, but the lighter its flavor.

Make sure you read the label to be certain the syrup is 100 percent: it is the only guarantee of quality. Keep the unopened bottle in a cool place, or at room temperature. Once opened, it is preferable to keep it in the refrigerator to slow down the crystallization process.

French toast
with pineapple marmalade and *viande des Grisons*

4 slices *viande des Grisons*
½ Victoria pineapple
3 tablespoons (1 ½ oz./40 g) butter
6 pink peppercorns, crushed
1 egg
Scant ½ cup (3 ½ fl. oz./100 ml) light cream
Salt and freshly ground white pepper
4 slices brioche
4 tablespoons sunflower oil

Cut the *viande des Grisons* into small pieces. Dice the pineapple.

In a non-stick skillet, heat half the butter and cook the pineapple pieces over a high heat for 5 minutes, until golden.

Combine the pineapple, the *viande des Grisons,* and the pink peppercorns in a bowl and set aside.

In a bowl, whisk the egg and cream together using a fork. Add a pinch of salt and a grinding of pepper. Dip the slices of brioche in this cream.

In a non-stick skillet, heat the oil and the remaining butter and fry the soaked slices of brioche on both sides until golden.

Transfer to warmed plates and top with the pineapple marmalade.

CHEF'S NOTE You can replace the *viande des Grisons* with bresaola, its Italian cousin, which is also made of beef.

FRUIT

PREPARATION TIME: 15 MINUTES • COOKING TIME: 40 MINUTES • SERVES 4

Apple, tomato, and mushroom clafoutis
with prosciutto

2 Golden Delicious apples

2 oz. (60 g) mushrooms

2 tablespoons (1 oz./30 g) butter

2 tomatoes (ideally Roma or Olivette), seeded and chopped

2 eggs

Scant 1 cup (7 fl. oz./200 ml) cream

Salt and freshly ground black pepper

2 slices prosciutto (San Daniele), shredded

Preheat the oven to 325°F/160°C/gas mark 3.

Peel the apples and cut into thick slices. Finely chop the mushrooms.

Heat a skillet and add a tablespoon of butter. Sauté the mushrooms for a few minutes, then add the apple slices along with another tablespoon of butter and cook for 5 minutes.

Add the tomatoes and cook for an additional 5 minutes.

Drain the vegetables, reserving the juice, and divide the vegetables between four ramekins.

Whisk the eggs with the cream. Add the liquid from the vegetables and season with salt and pepper. Pour the cream into the ramekins.

Place in the oven and cook for 20 minutes until the creams are set but still slightly wobbly.

Just before serving, top the ramekins with shredded prosciutto. Serve immediately.

CHEF'S NOTE San Daniele ham is a cured ham from Parma. It is produced in Friuli in northeastern Italy. World famous, it is made by artisan producers and has recognized legal status. Like all Parma hams, it should be sliced very finely for that melt-in-the-mouth texture.

Licorice, peaches, plums,
red currants, and rhubarb

2 peaches, pits removed, chopped

16 Mirabelle plums, pits removed, cut into quarters

2 tablespoons red currants

1 stick rhubarb, peeled and cut into slices

¼ cup (2 oz./60 g) brown sugar

Scant 1 cup (7 fl. oz./200 ml) apple juice

4 squares of Zan licorice candy, crushed to a powder

Combine all the ingredients in a large heatproof bowl. Cover with plastic wrap, making it as airtight as possible.

Place the bowl over a pot of simmering water (a bain-marie) and cook over a low heat for about 20 minutes (less if the fruits are very ripe).

When the fruit is stewed to a thick sauce, remove the plastic wrap, pour into a serving bowl, and allow to cool before serving.

CHEF'S NOTE Mirabelle plums are small sweet yellow plums, widely available in France. You can substitute other plums if Mirabelles are not available. Zan is a hard licorice candy from France.

Aloe vera, green mango,
and fennel with corn syrup and fresh cilantro

3 oz. (80 g) aloe vera, cubed

⅔ cup (3 ½ oz./100 g) dried apricots, chopped

3 ½ oz. (100 g) green mango flesh, cubed (about 1 mango)

3 oz. (80 g) fennel, finely chopped and soaked in cold water

Light corn syrup

7 oz. (200 g) tofu, cubed

4 tablespoons (10 g) cilantro leaves

In a large bowl, mix the aloe vera, apricots, mango, and drained fennel.

Sweeten with a little corn syrup and mix well.

Transfer to a serving bowl and add the tofu and the cilantro leaves just before serving.

Tao of avocado and fresh mango

2 ripe avocados, peeled, pitted, and roughly chopped

4 tablespoons sweetened condensed milk

⅓ cup (3 fl. oz./90 ml) crushed ice cubes

Zest and juice of 1 lime

11 oz. (320 g) fresh mango, cubed

In a blender, mix the avocado, condensed milk, crushed ice, and half of the lime juice (to prevent the avocado turning black) to make a smooth sauce. Place the cubes of mango in a small bowl and scatter over the lime zest and the remaining juice. Serve the avocado and mango separately, allowing guests to serve themselves.

Blood orange salad
with passionfruit and raisins

3 blood oranges

4 tablespoons golden raisins

2 tablespoons dark raisins

¼ cup (2 oz./60 g) passionfruit pulp

For the thickened orange juice:

2 cups (1 pint/500 ml) orange juice

2 tablespoons honey

Juice of 2 lemons

1 tablespoon (10 g) cornstarch

1 teaspoon (1 g) saffron threads

Peel the oranges, remove the pith, and cut the flesh into fine slices. Arrange in a large serving bowl and scatter over the raisins. Pour the passionfruit pulp over the top. To make the thickened orange juice, heat together the orange juice and the honey in a cooking pot. Mix the lemon juice and the cornstarch and pour this mixture slowly into the boiling orange juice. Cook over a medium heat, whisking continuously to thicken the mixture. Stir in the saffron threads. Pour the hot orange juice over the fruit in the serving bowl. Cover with plastic wrap and allow to cool before serving.

Fresh fruit salad
with aniseed syrup

For the aniseed syrup:

1 cup (½ pint/250 ml) mineral water

⅔ cup (4 ½ oz./125 g) sugar

1 vanilla bean, split

1 teaspoon black peppercorns

1 star anise

For the fresh fruit salad:

1 large slice watermelon, cubed

½ small melon, cubed

3 ½ oz. (100 g) strawberries, quartered

4 ½ oz. (125 g) raspberries, halved

1 ½ oz. (40 g) gooseberries

2 tablespoons lemon cordial (such as Pulco)

4 tablespoons Spiced syrup (see page 22)

3 tablespoons mature Kirsch (cherry liqueur)

Make the aniseed syrup a day before you want to serve the fruit salad. Put the water and the sugar in a large pot and bring to a boil. Add the vanilla, peppercorns, and star anise.

Cover tightly with plastic wrap and allow to infuse for 12 hours at room temperature.

Strain into a bottle and store in the refrigerator.

Carefully combine all the fruit for the fruit salad in a large serving bowl.

Add the lemon cordial and the spiced syrup, then the Kirsch, and stir gently to combine. Serve chilled, with the aniseed syrup.

PANCAKES, WAFFLES, CRÊPES, AND CO.

Waffles

There are two main types of waffle. The first, Brussels waffles, are made with a liquid batter like a crêpe batter, while the second, Liegeoise waffles, are made with a thicker batter that can be worked by hand to form little balls.

The cooking implement is the same for both types of waffles: the waffle iron, formed of two pieces of hinged metal between which the batter is placed to be cooked.

The inner face of the waffle iron is often decorated to give waffles their characteristic form.

The same type of iron has been used over the years to make hosts, round wafers, and other types of waffle. Modern waffle irons are electric, and sometimes come with removable plates so the waffle iron can be used to make *croque-monsieurs*.

Brussels waffle batter

Brussels, or Belgian, waffles are traditionally rectangular with 20 dimples. They used to be made without a rising agent, using instead melted butter to make them light and crispy. Adding baking powder gives an even lighter textured waffle.

3 ½ cups (12 oz./350 g) all-purpose flour
1 teaspoon baking powder
Pinch of salt
3 eggs, beaten
1 ½ cups (¾ pint/350 ml) milk
3 ½ tablespoons (1 ¾ oz./50 g) butter, melted

Sift the flour, baking powder, and salt into a large mixing bowl.

Make a well in the center and add the eggs. Using a whisk, start to incorporate the eggs into the flour.

Add the milk gradually and whisk in circular movements around the bowl, incorporating the flour a little at a time, until you have a smooth batter.

When all the flour has been incorporated, add the melted butter.

Allow the batter to rest for 10–15 minutes.

Cook in a waffle iron, following the manufacturer's instructions.

Serve immediately, with sugar on the side.

Liegeoise waffle batter

The Liegeoise waffle, or sugar waffle, is made with a fermented batter that contains a rising agent and cinnamon, and resembles a dough. This round waffle with 24 dimples is eaten warm.

¾ oz. (20g) fresh yeast
⅓ cup (3 fl. oz./90 ml) milk
1 tablespoon honey
1 vanilla bean, split
2 ½ cups (9 oz./250 g) all-purpose flour
1 egg

Pinch of salt
1 stick plus 1 tablespoon (4 oz./120 g) butter, softened
⅓ cup (3 oz./80 g) brown (beet) sugar, or Turbinado sugar

Dissolve the yeast in the milk with the honey and the vanilla seeds.

Place the flour in the bowl of a stand mixer and, using the dough hook on a low speed, add the milk, then the egg and the salt.

Increase the speed to knead the dough well.

Add half the butter and mix again.

Allow to rest for 20 minutes at room temperature.

Melt the remaining butter, add the sugar, and mix into the dough at low speed.

Allow to rest for 40 minutes.

Divide the dough into pats of about 2 oz. (60 g) each. Cook in the waffle iron, following the manufacturer's instructions, and serve immediately.

Serve with sugar and chantilly cream. Alternatively, try one of the following toppings, or the one on page 79—or invent your own.

CHOCOLATE WAFFLE Grate in some chocolate before forming the batter into balls.

CHEESE WAFFLE Flatten the uncooked waffle dough and place a little cheese in the middle. Fold over the edges to enclose the cheese, then cook in the waffle iron.

BACON WAFFLE As for the cheese waffle, but replace the cheese with a little cooked bacon.

Smoked herring and ham waffles

6 oz. (180 g) bean sprouts

1 smoked herring fillet

2 slices cured ham (Ardennes, if possible)

2 green apples

Juice of ½ lemon

Freshly ground white pepper

1 tablespoon walnut oil

6 Brussels waffles

3 ½ tablespoons sour cream, to serve

Clean the bean sprouts, and cut them into small pieces.

Cut the smoked herring, ham, and green apples into small dice.

Put the bean sprouts, herring, ham, and apple in a large bowl and stir gently to combine. Season with lemon juice and pepper and add the walnut oil.

Serve the waffles with a bowl of sour cream and the salad on the side.

Tandoori apple waffles

3 apples (cooking variety such as Reinette or Clochard)
½ stick (1 ¾ oz./50 g) butter
2 tablespoons brown sugar
½ tablespoon tandoori spice mix
6 Liegeoise waffles
Scant ½ cup (3 ½ fl. oz./100 ml) crème fraîche (farm fresh if possible—or sour cream)

Peel the apples and chop them into quarters.

Melt 2 tablespoons of the butter in a skillet and cook the apples until golden.

Sprinkle the sugar over, and allow to caramelize for 5 minutes over a low heat.

Add the remaining butter and the tandoori spice mix.

Divide the topping between the waffles and serve with crème fraîche.

Traditional blini batter

1 ½ cups (5 ½ oz./160 g) all-purpose flour
1 package dried instant yeast
2 eggs, separated
Scant ½ cup (3 ½ fl. oz./100 ml) warm water
1 teaspoon salt
½ cup (4 ¼ fl. oz./125 ml) plain yogurt
Butter

Combine the flour and the dried yeast. Stir in the egg yolks and the warm water, then the salt. Mix well.

Add the yogurt, and mix to make a smooth batter. Cover with plastic wrap and allow to rise in a warm place.

When the batter has doubled in volume, whip the egg whites in a separate bowl with a pinch of salt.

Combine the egg whites carefully into the batter.

To cook, heat a little butter in a large blini pan and cook spoonfuls of batter for 3 minutes on the first side, or until golden, before flipping and cooking the other side for 2 minutes. Once these blinis are cooked, set aside on a wire tray and continue to cook the remainder.

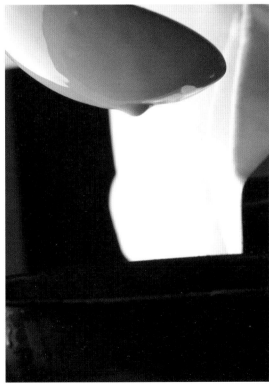

Crunchy white cabbage
and smoked salmon blinis

1 sweet white onion
¼ white cabbage
Salt
1 tablespoon white wine vinegar
Scant ½ cup (3 ½ fl. oz./100 ml) sour cream
2 smoked salmon slices, shredded
6 blinis, warm, to serve

Shred the onion and the cabbage using a mandoline.

Season with salt and vinegar and stir to combine. Gently mix in the sour cream, then turn out into a serving bowl.

Serve the cabbage salad, the smoked salmon, and the warm blinis separately.

Roast chicken
and salmon caviar blinis

Scant ½ cup (3 ½ oz./100 g) fresh *faisselle* cream cheese
   (cottage cheese may be substituted)
1 tablespoon snipped chives
Juice of ½ lemon
Salt and freshly ground white pepper
2 roast chicken breasts, cold
2 tablespoons (30 g) organic salmon caviar
1 tablespoon vodka
6 blinis, warm

Drain the fresh cream cheese and season with the chives, lemon juice, and salt and pepper.

Shred the chicken breasts. Sprinkle the salmon caviar with the vodka.

Serve the shredded chicken, the salmon caviar, and the flavored cheese in separate bowls alongside the warm blinis. Allow each guest to assemble their own blini by spreading a little fresh cheese, chicken, and salmon caviar on top.

Buckwheat pancakes

This traditional recipe from Brittany does not include eggs.

1 teaspoon coarse gray sea salt
2 ¾ cups (1 ½ pints/700 ml) cold mineral water
1 ¾ cups (10 ½ oz./300 g) buckwheat flour

Add the salt to the cold water, then whisk in the flour a little at a time until you have a thick batter. You may need a little more or less flour or water.

Use the batter immediately, cooking the pancakes in a heavy-bottomed skillet (known as a "galetier" in French). You will need 3–4 tablespoons (20–30 g) of batter per pancake (they should not be too thick).

Blood sausage and applesauce pancakes

Salted butter
4 buckwheat pancakes
Scant ½ cup (3 ½ oz./100 g) applesauce

12 slices blood sausage
Freshly ground black pepper

Grease a skillet with a little butter and heat.

Place a cooked buckwheat pancake on the skillet, spread with a little more butter, then flip over.

Spread over the applesauce and three slices of sausage. Fold over the edges of the pancakes to make a square parcel, then turn over and cook for 2 minutes. Serve immediately.

Onion and Camembert pancakes

Salted butter

11 oz. (300 g) sweet pink onions, finely chopped

Salt and freshly ground black pepper

4 buckwheat pancakes

½ Camembert, sliced

Melt 2 tablespoons of butter in a pot, add the chopped onions, and sweat them. Season lightly with salt, add ½ cup of water, and cook for an additional 10 minutes. Process the cooked onions to make a thick purée.

Heat a greased skillet, place a pancake in the skillet, spread with a little more butter, and flip over the pancake. Spread a little of the onion purée on the pancake and add a few slices of Camembert. Season generously with black pepper. Fold up the edges of the pancake to make a square parcel, then flip over and cook for an additional 2 minutes. Serve immediately.

Moroccan "thousand-hole" crêpes

1 ½ cups (9 oz./250 g) fine couscous

Scant 2 cups (1 pint/450 ml) warm water

½ teaspoon salt

Pinch of baking powder

1 package dried instant yeast

2 tablespoons sunflower oil

Pour the couscous into a bowl, make a well in the center, and add all the other ingredients. Process for 3 minutes with a stick blender to make a batter. Cover the bowl with plastic wrap, and allow to rest for 30 minutes in a warm place.

Using a lightly-oiled non-stick skillet, cook the crêpes one at a time until holes start to form on the surface. Remove to a plate, cover with a clean dish towel, and continue until all the batter is used. Serve hot with a mixture of honey and melted butter, one of the toppings on the following page, or with whatever else takes your fancy.

Fresh goat cheese crêpes
with honey and almonds

2 tablespoons fresh goat cheese

Juice of ½ lemon

Salt and freshly ground white pepper

3 tablespoons slivered almonds

4 teaspoons strawberry-tree honey

8 Moroccan "thousand-hole" crêpes

Mix the goat cheese with the lemon juice and season.

Toast the almonds in a small skillet, and set aside on a plate.

Place a spoonful of cheese on each crêpe. Drizzle over a little honey and top with toasted almonds. Serve immediately.

Foie gras crêpes
with almonds and apricots

2 slices foie gras, cooked

2 piquillo peppers

8 dried apricots

8 Moroccan "thousand-hole" crêpes

2 tablespoons sweet mustard

2 tablespoons chestnut honey

Freshly ground black pepper

Mash the foie gras. Cut the piquillo peppers and dried apricots into small dice.

Spread the pancakes with the mustard, top with a little foie gras, and sprinkle with a spoonful of the apricot–piquillo mixture.

Drizzle over a little honey and season with pepper.

Pancakes

2 ¾ cups (10 oz./280 g) all-purpose flour

1 teaspoon baking powder

1 teaspoon salt

1 teaspoon demerara sugar

2 cups (1 pint/500 ml) milk

3 eggs, beaten

4 tablespoons melted butter

Olive oil

Maple syrup or corn syrup to taste

Sift together the flour, baking powder, and salt in a mixing bowl, then stir in the sugar.

Make a well in the center and pour in the milk and the beaten eggs.

Combine well then add the melted butter little by little.

Heat a drop of olive oil in a small blini pan. Pour in a small ladleful of mixture and cook for 2–3 minutes, until small bubbles form on the surface of the pancakes. Flip over and continue to cook until golden brown.

Remove from the pan, set aside on a large plate, and continue to cook the remaining pancakes. Just before serving, drizzle over the maple syrup.

GRILLED SANDWICHES

The idea is the same no matter what the filler: heat up the waffle iron with sandwich plates (or toasted sandwich maker), butter two slices of bread, place in the waffle iron, and spread each one with a filling. Top each sandwich with a second, buttered slice of bread and close the waffle iron. Cook for 4–5 minutes, following the manufacturer's instructions. Take out the grilled sandwiches and eat immediately. Watch out though—they'll be hot!

Try the following sweet grilled sandwich ideas:

Brioche bread, grated dark chocolate, 1 large spoonful of lemon marmalade

Sandwich bread, 1 spoonful of caramel spread, 1 large spoonful of orange marmalade

Brioche bread, 1 spoonful of chestnut purée, 1 dash of crème fraîche (or sour cream), 1 pinch of crushed pistachios

FRUIT JUICES, DRINKS, INFUSIONS

PREPARATION TIME: 15 MINUTES • MAKES ABOUT 8 ½ CUPS (4 ¼ PINTS/2 LITERS)

Red berry juice

1 lb. (500 g) strawberries
½ lb. (250 g) raspberries
7 oz. (200 g) cherries, pitted
3 oz. (80 g) red currants

1 ½ tablespoons lemon juice
¾ cup (5 oz./150 g) white granulated sugar
Mineral water
Crushed ice, to serve

Process all the fruits with the lemon juice and sugar in a food processor to make a smooth purée. Push the purée through a fine sieve to extract the maximum juice possible. Thin out the pulp with some mineral water until you have a drinkable texture. Serve with crushed ice. Keep in a cool place.

PREPARATION TIME: 10 MINUTES • MAKES ABOUT 4 ¼ CUPS (2 PINTS/1 LITER)

Tomato, watermelon, and basil juice

2 ½ cups (1 ¼ pints/600 ml) tomato juice
1 lb. (500 g) watermelon flesh
Scant ½ cup (3 ½ fl. oz./100 ml) mineral water

¼ cup (1 ¾ oz./50 g) white granulated sugar
4 tablespoons basil leaves
Salt and freshly ground white pepper

Process together the tomato juice, watermelon, mineral water, sugar, and basil leaves. Pass through a sieve and season with salt and pepper.

PREPARATION TIME: 15 MINUTES • MAKES ABOUT 4 ¼ CUPS (2 PINTS/1 LITER)

Melon and strawberry fizz

1 lb. (500 g) watermelon flesh
½ lb. (250 g) strawberries
1 lb. (500 g) melon

2 tablespoons lemon juice
2 cups (1 pint/500 ml) carbonated water

Cut all the fruit into cubes and mix in a food processor with the lemon juice until you have a smooth purée. Filter the purée through a fine sieve. Thin out the resulting purée with the carbonated water. Serve chilled.

Blood orange, prune,
lemon, and passionfruit juice

10 passionfruits

Juice of 8 oranges

2 cups (1 pint/500 ml) prune juice

Juice of 3 lemons

Cut the passionfruits in half and remove the pulp using a spoon. Combine with all the fruit juices and serve chilled.

Fresh grape juice, papaya,
and coconut milk with ginger

5 oz. (150 g) Muscat grapes

1 papaya

1 tablespoon grated fresh ginger

Scant 1 cup (7 fl. oz./200 ml) coconut milk

Ice, to serve

Push the grapes through a fine sieve to extract the juice. Peel and seed the papaya. Place the papaya flesh with the grape juice and the ginger in the food processor and mix to a smooth purée. Whisk the resulting juice together with the coconut milk and serve with ice.

Pink grapefruit, carrot,
and pear juice

2 pink grapefruits
Scant ½ cup (3 ½ fl. oz./100 ml) pear nectar
Scant 1 cup (7 fl. oz./200 ml) carrot juice

Squeeze the grapefruit. Mix the three juices together and drink chilled.

Leek broth with seaweed
and bonito flakes

5 oz. (150 g) green part of leek, finely chopped
1 oz. (30 g) black radish, diced
4 ¼ cups (2 pints/1 liter) mineral water

Pinch of kosher salt
1 small piece of kombu seaweed
1 oz. (30 g) bonito flakes

Put the leek and radish in a large pot with the water and bring to a boil over a low heat. Turn down the heat and allow to simmer, without boiling, for 15 minutes, skimming off any impurities that rise to the surface. Remove from the heat, and add the salt, seaweed, and bonito flakes. Cover tightly with plastic wrap and allow to infuse until the broth is completely cold.

Filter the broth through a cloth, without pressing on the vegetables. Store in a glass bottle with a stopper in the refrigerator.

CHEF'S NOTE You can drink this sea-scented infusion as it is, warm or cold, or use it as a base for many other recipes.

Chilled verbena infusion
with citrus flavors

1 organic orange	4 ¼ cups (2 pints/1 liter) mineral water
1 organic lemon	¾ cup (5 oz./150 g) white granulated sugar
1 organic lime	¾ oz. (20 g) fresh verbena leaves

Slice the citrus fruits finely. Bring the water and sugar to a boil together in a large pot. Add the verbena leaves and the citrus slices. Remove from the heat, pour into a bowl, and cover tightly with plastic wrap. Allow to cool to room temperature, then move to the refrigerator and allow to infuse for an additional 12 hours. Strain through a fine sieve, and store the liquid in the refrigerator.

Vegetable infusion

5 oz. (150 g) green part of leek	2 sticks lemongrass
3 ½ oz. (90 g) carrots	1 bunch lemon balm leaves, crushed
3 oz. (80 g) turnips	4 ¼ cups (2 pints/1 liter) mineral water
2 oz. (60 g) fennel	2 teaspoons salt
1 ¾ oz. (50 g) celery	

Finely chop all the vegetables and the lemongrass. Place all the ingredients in a large stainless steel pot. Add the mineral water and salt and bring to a boil, skimming off any impurities that rise to the surface. Remove from the heat, pour into a bowl, and cover tightly with plastic wrap. Allow to cool completely, then strain carefully through a cloth, pressing only lightly on the vegetables. Store in the refrigerator.

CHEF'S NOTE You can drink this infusion hot or cold.

Orange and cardamom coffee

2 cardamom pods
½ cup (1 ¾ oz./50 g) finely ground coffee
  (Arabic or Turkish)

⅛ cup (1 ¾ oz./50 g) sugar
Finely grated zest of 1 organic orange
2 cups (1 pint/500 ml) mineral water

Crush the cardamom pods, and remove the seeds. Place the coffee, sugar, cardamom seeds, and orange zest in a small pot. Add the water and stir well. Bring to a boil, then remove from the heat for a minute. Bring back to a boil for a second time, then remove from the heat. Repeat a third time, then pour the coffee into coffee cups. Allow the coffee to stand for 5 minutes before drinking to allow the grounds to fall to the bottom of the cup.

CHEF'S NOTE For a classic "long" American coffee, mix the cardamom seeds with the ground coffee, add the orange zest, then place this mixture in a filter coffee machine.

If you love the flavor of cardamom in your coffee, place several crushed pods in your coffee package for at least a week.

Canada Dry® mojito

¼ cup (1 ¾ oz./50 g) sugar
½ cup (1 oz./30 g) snipped mint leaves
Zest of 2 limes
Ice

Juice of 2 pink grapefruits
½ cup (4 ¼ fl. oz./125 ml) Canada Dry® (or lemonade)
3 tablespoons grenadine syrup

In a large bowl, mash together the sugar, mint, and lime zest. Transfer to a large pitcher and add some ice. Pour in the grapefruit juice and Canada Dry®, and then add the grenadine. Pour into small glasses and serve chilled.

Hot chocolate

4 ½ oz. (125 g) dark chocolate (bitterness to taste)

2 cups (1 pint/500 ml) mineral water

⅓ cup (1 ¾ oz./50 g) muscovado sugar (brown sugar may be substituted)

3 ½ tablespoons (25 g) cocoa powder

1 pinch of ground coffee

Chop the dark chocolate with a sharp knife and place in a small pot.

Bring the mineral water to a boil in a separate pot.

Mix the sugar, cocoa powder, and coffee in a high-sided bowl.

Mix the boiling water little by little into this mixture, using a stick blender. When the mixture is smooth, pour it over the chopped chocolate.

Allow to rest for 5 minutes, then place the pot over a low heat and cook gently, stirring all the time, for 5 minutes, until the mixture is creamy.

Just before serving, froth the hot chocolate with the stick blender and serve immediately.

CHEF'S NOTE Muscovado is a brown unrefined cane sugar, available from specialty suppliers. It is also known as Barbados sugar.

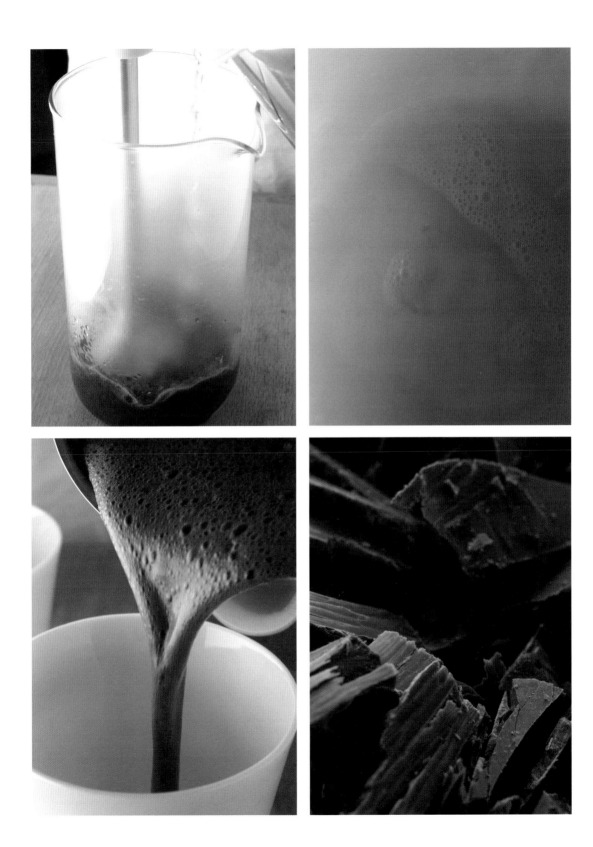

LUNCH

Hot and Cold Sandwiches

Cold Meats

Soups

HOT AND COLD SANDWICHES

PREPARATION TIME: 15 MINUTES • SERVES 4

Pita feast

4 pita breads

4 tablespoons Zucchini pesto (see page 106)

6 anchovy fillets in oil

2 hard-boiled eggs, finely chopped

1 iceberg lettuce, shredded

2 mushrooms, finely chopped

½ cup (3 ½ oz./100 g) corn

8 slices mortadella, shredded

Freshly ground black pepper

Warm the pitas for 20 seconds in the microwave, then split them open.

Spread the zucchini pesto on the insides, add the anchovy fillets and the chopped, hard-boiled eggs. Add a little lettuce, and some mushrooms, corn, and shredded mortadella.

Season with pepper, close, and serve immediately.

"Big Benat" sandwich

4 round sweet buns

2 tablespoons olive oil

7 oz. (200 g) ham, diced

½ tablespoon sesame oil

4 tablespoons Korean sauce, available from specialist stores

Freshly ground black pepper

1 beefheart tomato, thinly sliced

1 onion, sliced into rings

¾ oz. (20 g) *pain d'épices*, or gingerbread, crushed into crumbs

¼ cup (1 ½ oz./40 g) sundried tomatoes

1 large handful of arugula

Split the buns open, drizzle with half the olive oil, and toast until golden.

In a skillet, sauté the ham briefly in the sesame oil. Add the Korean sauce, season well with freshly ground black pepper, and remove to a plate.

Add the tomato to the skillet and sauté briefly, then remove to a plate.

Sauté the onion in the remaining olive oil, then add the gingerbread crumbs.

To make your sandwich, place a slice of tomato on the bottom half of each bun, and arrange a little ham and the sundried tomatoes on top. Add the onions. Season with pepper and top with a few arugula leaves.

Put the tops on the buns, holding them in place with a long toothpick, and serve immediately.

CHEF'S NOTE Korean sauce is a thick and fruity brown sauce with a texture like ketchup. The Japanese Bull-Dog sauce may be substituted.

Haddock taramasalata bagels

Scant ½ cup (1 oz./25 g) fresh bread crumbs

1 tablespoon milk

3 ½ oz. (100 g) haddock

Scant ½ cup (3 ½ fl. oz./100 ml) peanut oil

3 ½ tablespoons olive oil

1 lemon

Salt and pepper

4 bagels

2 ½ oz. (60 g) celery, finely chopped

To prepare the taramasalata, put the bread crumbs in a bowl and add the milk to soak the crumbs.

Cut the haddock into small cubes and place in the bowl of a food processor. Process to a paste, then add the soaked bread crumbs.

Process again, adding the peanut oil in a steady stream, then the olive oil, and finally the juice of half the lemon. Check the seasoning.

Remove the mixture to a small bowl and set aside in the refrigerator.

When ready to serve, split the bagels open and toast them, then spread with taramasalata. Scatter over the chopped celery, add a few drops of lemon juice, put the tops on the bagels, and serve immediately.

Zucchini pesto

1 large zucchini
3 tablespoons (25 g) pine nuts
5 basil sprigs
1 garlic clove, crushed
Scant ½ cup (3 ½ fl. oz./100 ml) olive oil
Salt and freshly ground black pepper

Fill a large pot with water and bring to a boil. Chop the zucchini into large chunks, place in the boiling water, and cook for 10 minutes.

When cooked through, drain the zucchini and refresh under cold running water, then drain again well.

Put the zucchini in the bowl of a food processor with the pine nuts, basil leaves, and garlic, and process until you have a smooth paste. Add the olive oil in a steady stream. Season with salt and pepper.

Keep in a jar in the refrigerator until ready to use. It can be kept for 3–4 days.

Otti tomato sauce

2 lb. (1 kg) ripe tomatoes

5 oz. (150 g) onions, finely chopped

1 tablespoon olive oil

1½ oz. (40 g) lemongrass (about 3 stalks),
   chopped into large pieces

2 tablespoons finely grated fresh ginger

Generous 1 cup (9 fl. oz./250 ml)
   thick coconut milk

⅔ cup (1¾ oz./50 g) shredded coconut

Salt

Blanch the tomatoes briefly in boiling water. Drain, skin, and seed them, then chop roughly.

In a large skillet, sweat the onions gently in the olive oil, without allowing them to color.

Add the chopped tomatoes, lemongrass, ginger, and coconut milk and simmer over a low heat for 1 hour, stirring regularly, until you have a thick sauce.

Remove the lemongrass and discard. Add the shredded coconut, and check the seasoning.

Remove from the heat and keep in the refrigerator until needed. It can be kept for 3–4 days.

Otti tomato bagels

1 large beefheart tomato

⅓ cup (1¾ oz./50 g) sundried tomatoes

4 bagels

7 oz. (200 g) Otti tomato sauce (see above)

1 bunch lemon balm

Cut the beefheart tomato into slices, and each slice in half. Chop the dried tomatoes.

Warm the bagels, and split them open. Spread with otti tomato sauce and place the slices of beefheart and dried tomatoes on top. Garnish with lemon balm leaves, put the top on the bagels, and serve immediately.

Beef tataki
with Krisprolls®

Sunflower oil
1 skirt steak
¾ oz. (15 g) cooked beet
1 ½ tablespoons soy sauce
1 ½ tablespoons cornstarch
5 teaspoons mirin
2 tablespoons sake
5 drops of sesame oil
1 scallion, finely chopped
1 tablespoon toasted sesame seeds
Pinch of Sichuan pepper
10 Krisprolls®, or small slices toasted bread

Heat a non-stick skillet with a drop of sunflower oil. When the skillet is very hot, sear the steak briefly on each side, so it remains rare. Place the cooked meat on absorbent paper towels and set aside in the refrigerator.

Process the beet with the soy sauce. Dissolve the cornstarch in the mirin and add this to the beet. Cook gently for 1 minute over a low heat to make a smooth sauce.

Allow to cool, then add the sake and the sesame oil, whisking to keep the sauce smooth.

Slice the meat finely and place in a serving dish, then combine with a little sauce and the chopped scallion. Sprinkle with the toasted sesame seeds and the Sichuan pepper.

Serve the tataki, chilled, with warmed Krisprolls® or toasted slices of country bread.

CHEF'S NOTE Mirin is a fermented rice alcohol that is less strong in taste than sake and sometimes has a plum flavor. It is widely available in Asian markets.

Duck club sandwiches
with Provolone

12 slices sandwich bread
1 duck breast
Salt and freshly ground black pepper
8 thin slices Provolone cheese

For the relish:
⅓ cup (2 ¾ oz./30 g) pistachios
1 ¼ cups (10 fl. oz./300 ml) prune juice, hot
2 tablespoons white wine vinegar
1 tablespoon olive oil
1 teaspoon dry mustard powder (e.g. Colman's)
Salt

Preheat the oven to 300°F/150°C/gas mark 2.

Cut the crusts off the bread and discard. Roll the crustless bread slices with a rolling pin to flatten them out. Place on a baking sheet and dry in the oven for 30 minutes.

Meanwhile make the relish: process the pistachios with the hot prune juice, then add the white wine vinegar and the olive oil. Add the mustard powder and season lightly with salt.

Rub the duck breast with salt and freshly ground black pepper. Heat a skillet, and add a drop of water (this will help the duck fat to melt without burning). Cook the duck breast, skin-side down, for 8 minutes, removing the melted fat as you go. Turn over and cook for an additional 5 minutes.

Remove to a plate and allow to rest for a few minutes before shredding the duck breast. Transfer to a bowl, add the relish and stir to combine.

Place a slice of provolone on eight of the toast slices. Return to the oven to melt the cheese. Scatter the relish-covered shredded duck breast over four of the cheese-covered toast slices and season generously with pepper.

Add another slice of cheese-covered toast, and repeat the filling, then top with the remaining slices of toast. Serve immediately.

Mango and piquillo pepper
sandwich

1 large tomato

½ yellow mango

2 piquillo peppers, from a jar

10 black olives

2 tablespoons olive oil

Salt and freshly ground black pepper

4 slices country-style bread (e.g. Poilâne)

1 garlic clove, peeled and cut in half

8 thin slices speck (smoked cured ham)

Blanch, skin, and seed the tomato. Cut the flesh into cubes.

Cut the mango and the piquillo peppers into the same size cubes.

Pit the olives and slice them thinly.

Combine the tomato, mango, piquillo peppers, and olives in a bowl, add a splash of olive oil, and season with salt.

Toast the slices of bread and rub lightly with the cut garlic clove.

Spread a spoonful of vegetable mixture on each slice and top with two speck slices. Season with pepper and serve immediately.

CHEF'S NOTE Poilâne bread is a sourdough country bread.

Shiitake mushroom and Gorgonzola
ciabatta

6 large shiitake mushrooms

Salt and freshly ground black pepper

1 tablespoon soy sauce

3 tablespoons olive oil

4 ciabatta breads

5 oz. (150 g) Gorgonzola cheese, crumbled

1 handful arugula

Remove the stems from the mushrooms and discard. Place the mushrooms head-down in a large non-stick skillet and sprinkle with salt. Place a pot on the top as a weight. Cook for 5 minutes then remove the pot and turn over the mushrooms. Replace the pot on the mushrooms and continue to cook for another 8 minutes. Remove the mushrooms from the pan and place on a dish. Sprinkle with soy sauce, olive oil, and pepper. Heat the broiler oven. Split the ciabattas, brush some olive oil over the insides and toast in the broiler oven for 5 minutes. Chop the mushrooms finely and divide them between the ciabatta toasts, then scatter with crumbled Gorgonzola. Return to the oven for a few minutes to melt the cheese. Season with pepper, garnish with arugula, put the tops on, and serve immediately.

Fresh anchovy open-faced
sandwiches

11 oz. (300 g) fresh anchovies, cleaned

2 cups (1 pint/500 ml) mineral water

5 tablespoons dry white wine

Table salt

Scant ½ cup (3 ½ fl. oz./100 ml) olive oil

2 garlic cloves, sliced

1 hot chili pepper

½ red bell pepper, seeded and diced

8 slices country-style bread, toasted

Split open the anchovies and remove all the bones. Pour the water and white wine into a large bowl and season lightly with salt. Rinse the anchovies carefully in this liquid then drain them and dry with absorbent paper towels. Place the anchovies in a shallow dish. Heat the olive oil in a skillet, add the sliced garlic and chili pepper, then pour this flavored oil over the anchovies. Scatter the diced sweet red pepper over the top, and allow to cool to room temperature. Pile onto the slices of toast and serve.

Reblochon cheese open-faced
sandwiches flambéed with génépi liqueur

4 slices multigrain bread

2 tablespoons crème fraîche (or sour cream)

1 teaspoon strong mustard

Salt and freshly ground black pepper

¼ Reblochon cheese

1 small glass of génépi liqueur (similar to Chartreuse)

Preheat the oven to 300°F/150°C/gas mark 2. Toast the bread.

Mix the crème fraîche and the mustard and season lightly with salt. Spread this mixture onto the toasted bread.

Cut the cheese into thick slices and place on top. Warm in the oven for a few minutes.

Heat the génépi in a small pot.

Place the open sandwiches on a serving plate, pour over the génépi, and flambé just before serving.

CHEF'S NOTE Génépi is a liqueur with similar ingredients to absinthe. Chartreuse is similar, a French liqueur that has been made by Carthusian monks since the 1740s. It is made from distilled alcohol flavored with 130 herbal extracts.

Dried flatbread, sea bream
with sake, and heart of palm cocktail

2 slices flatbread (about 11¾ x 7¾ in. / 30 x 20 cm)

2 sea bream fillets

3 tablespoons olive oil

Scant ½ cup (3 ½ fl. oz./100 ml) coconut water

1 tablespoon sake

Juice and zest of 1 lime

Pink peppercorns, crushed

Kosher salt

3 tablespoons mayonnaise

4 tablespoons mineral water

A few drops green Tabasco

1 can of heart of palm, finely chopped

Preheat the oven to 325°F/160°C/gas mark 3.

Place one slice of flatbread on top of the other and cut into four large squares. Dry out in the oven for 20 minutes.

Place the sea bream fillets on a sheet of plastic wrap and put in the freezer until frozen.

Remove from the freezer, allow to defrost slightly, then cut into large cubes and place in a large mixing bowl.

Add the olive oil, coconut water, sake, and lime juice and zest. Season with the crushed pink peppercorns and a little kosher salt and turn carefully to combine.

Place the mayonnaise in a separate bowl, and mix in the mineral water to thin it out. Season it lightly with salt and green Tabasco. Add the heart of palm and combine carefully.

Place the heart of palm mayonnaise in four short glasses. Set aside in the refrigerator until needed.

When ready to serve, spread the marinated sea bream tartare on the flatbread (keeping the double layer), sprinkle with salt, and place a slice on top of each glass. Serve immediately.

COLD MEATS

Mortadella platter

11 oz. (300 g) celeriac, peeled and diced

7 oz. (200 g) green beans

3 ½ tablespoons light cream

4 teaspoons strong mustard

2 tablespoons (1 ½ oz./40 g) Mostarda di Cremona, in ⅛ in. (3 mm) dice

2 ½ oz. (60 g) turnip, in ⅛ in. (3 mm) dice

Salt and freshly ground white pepper

Olive oil

6 oz. (180 g) finely sliced mortadella

1 ball mozzarella (5 ½ oz./160 g), finely sliced

Cook the celeriac in boiling salted water until cooked through.

Cook the green beans in boiling salted water until al dente. Drain, refresh, and set aside.

Drain the cooked celeriac and mash with the cream. Allow to cool.

When it has cooled down, mix in the strong mustard and the Mostarda di Cremona. Divide between four small bowls and set aside.

Season separately the turnips and the green beans with salt, pepper, and olive oil.

Place the mortadella on flat plates, and arrange the mozzarella, green beans, and raw turnip on top.

Serve, with the celeriac purée in a separate bowl.

CHEF'S NOTE Mostarda di Cremona is an Italian condiment made from fruits (cherries, pears, oranges, plum, melon, fig, and vegetable marrow) preserved in a syrup flavored with essential oil of mustard.

Chicken breast with anchovies

4 skinless chicken breasts
Salt and freshly ground white pepper
Pinch of fresh thyme flowers
4 tablespoons sesame oil
7 oz. (200 g) fresh tomatoes
4 tablespoons lemon juice
8 anchovies, cut lengthwise

Split open the chicken breasts lengthwise and place between two sheets of plastic wrap. Beat with a rolling pin until you have four fine scallops.

Place in a shallow dish and season with salt, pepper, thyme flowers, and sesame oil. Allow to marinate for 10–15 minutes.

Meanwhile, roughly chop the tomatoes and add the lemon juice, salt, and pepper. Place in a food processor and mix to make a juice, then strain through a fine sieve. Set aside.

Cook the chicken breasts over a medium heat in a non-stick skillet. When cooked through, place directly onto serving plates and allow to cool to room temperature.

Arrange the anchovy strips on top of the chicken breasts and then pour over the tomato juice.

SOUPS

PREPARATION TIME: 15 MINUTES · INFUSION TIME: 1 HOUR
COOKING TIME: 5 MINUTES · SERVES 4

Coconut and mushroom broth

1 cup (9 fl. oz./250 ml) dry white wine

2 lb. (1 kg) small white mushrooms, finely chopped

4 ½ cups (2 pints/1 liter) spring water

Scant ½ cup (7 fl. oz./100 ml) sweet white wine

1 cup (9 oz./250 g) thick coconut milk, or coconut cream (unsweetened)

1 tablespoon soy sauce

1 tablespoon mustard

1 stick (3 ½ oz./100 g) butter, chilled

1 bunch fresh herbs, such as parsley, chervil, chives, dill

4 slices sandwich bread

Pepper

In a large pot, bring the dry white wine to a boil and add the mushrooms. Stir, add the spring water, sweet white wine, coconut cream, and soy sauce.

Bring back to a boil, remove from the heat, and cover tightly with plastic wrap. Allow to infuse for 1 hour.

Pass through a sieve, reserving both broth and mushrooms. Place the chopped mushrooms in a small bowl and season with the mustard. Set aside.

Pour the broth into a blender and, with the motor running, add the chilled butter and the herbs and mix on a medium speed to emulsify. Return to the pan and reheat.

Toast the bread and top each slice with a spoonful of mushrooms. Serve with the hot broth.

Cream of foie gras soup

½ lb. (200 g) raw duck foie gras
Scant ½ cup (3 ½ fl. oz./100 ml) red port
2 cups (1 pint/500 ml) tasty chicken broth
Salt and freshly ground pepper

Push the raw foie gras through a fine sieve using the back of a wooden spoon. Set aside the resulting purée in the refrigerator.

In a pot, bring the port to a boil, flambé it, then cook until it is reduced by half.

Add the chicken broth to the reduced port, and bring back to a boil.

Using a stick blender, mix the broth to emulsify it, and add the foie gras purée a little at a time until you have a smooth soup. Check the seasoning and serve immediately.

CHEF'S NOTE Do not reboil this soup. If you need to heat it up later, do so over a bain-marie or at a low heat in the microwave.

Sketch popcorn soup

This recipe reminds me of my meeting with Mourad Mazouz and the creation of Sketch in Mayfair, London.

3 fresh ears of corn
2 cups (1 pint/500 ml) whole milk
2 cups (1 pint/500 ml) mineral water
Salt and freshly ground black pepper
Scant ½ cup (3 ½ oz./100 g) Philadelphia cream cheese
2 ¾ oz./80 g salted popcorn

Scrape the fresh corn off the ears with a sharp knife, and cook the kernels over a low heat in the milk and water. Season lightly with salt.

Drain the corn, reserving the cooking liquid, and place in the bowl of a food processor. Process, adding the cooking liquid little by little until smooth. Check the seasoning.

Strain through a fine sieve, pushing down well on the corn.

At the table, place a heaping spoonful of Philadelphia in the center of each of four warmed soup bowls, and pour over the soup, scattering over the popcorn to garnish.

Andy's tomato soup
(in homage to Andy Warhol)

2 tablespoons olive oil

9 oz. (250 g) onions, finely chopped

Salt and freshly ground black pepper

2 tablespoons tomato paste

1 ¾ lb. (800 g) tomatoes, roughly chopped

3 ½ oz. (100 g) celery, chopped

2 garlic cloves

1 sugar lump

3 cups (1 ½ pints/750 ml) spring water

1 thyme sprig

2 bay leaves

1 can sardines in oil

Tabasco

1 tablespoon vodka

Heat the oil in a pot and sauté the onions until golden brown. Season with salt, then add the tomato paste and cook for an additional 3–4 minutes.

Add the tomatoes, celery, garlic, and sugar. Allow to cook down for a few minutes, then add the water, thyme, and bay leaves. Cook over a low heat for about 30 minutes until thick.

Remove the thyme and bay leaves, then purée the soup, using a stick blender, until smooth. Push the soup through a fine sieve using the back of the spoon.

In a bowl, mash the drained sardines and add the Tabasco and vodka. Form the mixture into four little balls.

Pour the soup into four warmed bowls, drop a sardine ball into each bowl ... and enjoy!

Jerusalem artichoke soup
with sorrel

1 lb. (500 g) Jerusalem artichokes
4 ¼ cups (2 pints/1 liter) milk
Salt and freshly ground white pepper
2 tablespoons (1 oz./30 g) butter
4 oz. (120 g) sorrel leaves, finely chopped
⅔ cup (5 fl. oz./150 ml) cream

Peel, wash, and chop the Jerusalem artichokes.

Place the milk in a large cooking pot and season lightly with salt and pepper. Drop in the chopped artichokes and simmer until cooked through. Drain the artichokes, reserving the cooking liquid.

Meanwhile, in another pot, melt the butter and add the sorrel. Season with salt and cook for 3–4 minutes. Remove from the heat and set aside.

Bring the cream to a boil. Process the artichokes to a purée with the hot cream. Add the reserved cooking liquid a little at a time to make a smooth soup. Check the seasoning.

Put the soup back on the heat to warm through. Just before serving, remove from the heat and mix in the cooked sorrel. Serve in a soup tureen or in individual soup bowls.

Mussel soup
with turmeric

1 shallot, finely chopped
2 glasses white wine (Chardonnay)
2 tablespoons (1 oz./30 g) butter
14 oz. (400g) mussels, cleaned, beards removed
1 cup (½ pint/250 ml) light cream
½ teaspoon turmeric
Salt and freshly ground white pepper

Put the shallot in a large pot with the white wine and half the butter. Bring to a boil.

Place the cleaned mussels in the pot, cover, and cook for 5 minutes. Remove from the heat and allow to rest for 5 minutes.

Drain the mussels. Reserve the cooking liquid, and strain it through a fine sieve. Remove the mussels from their shells.

Return the cooking liquid to the pot and add the cream. Reduce for 5 minutes.

Add the turmeric and half of the shelled mussels and process with a stick blender, adding the rest of the butter as you go. Check the seasoning.

Divide the remaining mussels between warmed soup bowls, pour over the soup, and serve immediately.

DINNER

APPETIZERS

PREPARATION TIME: 25 MINUTES · FREEZING TIME: 15 MINUTES · SERVES 4

Raw langoustine rice-paper rolls

16 langoustine tails

Salt and freshly ground white pepper

1 tablespoon dry white wine

Piment d'Espelette, or hot paprika

Juice of 1 lemon

2 tablespoons grated fresh ginger

1 tablespoon nuoc mam (fish sauce)

4 tablespoons sesame oil

1 tablespoon snipped garlic chives

1 ripe avocado

3 oz. (80 g) Thai grapefruit or pomelo, chopped

4 tablespoons young herbs, such as shiso, cilantro, etc.

1 scallion, snipped

4 round rice papers

Peel the langoustine tails and cut into large chunks. Season with salt, pepper, and the white wine. Sprinkle with some *piment d'Espelette* and place in the freezer so that they are very well chilled.

In a bowl, mix the lemon juice, grated ginger, nuoc mam, sesame oil, garlic chives, salt, and some *piment d'Espelette*.

Peel, pit, and dice the avocado and place in a bowl with the chopped Thai grapefruit. Spoon over one spoonful of this sauce, keeping the rest to serve with the dish (the rolls can be dipped in the sauce). Scatter over half of the young herbs and the scallion, and set aside in the refrigerator.

Soften the rice papers by soaking for 1 minute in hot water, then spread them out on a clean cloth.

Place a spoonful of the avocado–grapefruit mixture in the center of each rice paper, add some cubes of langoustine, and roll up the rice papers.

Serve immediately on cold plates, sprinkled with the remaining young herbs.

CHEF'S NOTE Frozen langoustines may be used; in this case, cut them into chunks when frozen and season.

Michel Nave's stuffed eggplants

2 eggplants
Salt and freshly ground black pepper
Olive oil
3 ½ oz. (100 g) smoked bacon, diced
7 oz. (200 g) onions, finely chopped
1 green bell pepper, diced
8 ½ cups (4 ¼ pints/2 liters) water
1 thyme sprig
2 bay leaves

For the stuffing:
2 ½ oz. (60 g) shallots, finely chopped
1 garlic clove, finely chopped
7 oz. (200 g) tomatoes, diced
1 tablespoon snipped parsley
2 tablespoons snipped chives
4 oz. (120 g) piquillo peppers from a jar,
   cut into ⅛ in. (3 mm) dice
¼ cup (1 oz./30 g) pine nuts, toasted and crushed
Scant ½ cup (3 ½ oz./100 g) lean ground lamb

Cut the eggplants into 1 ½ in. (4 cm) slices. Carve a small hollow 1 ½ in. (4 cm) in diameter by ¾ in. (2 cm) deep in each slice. Sprinkle with salt, and allow to stand for 30 minutes. Finely chop the eggplant trimmings.

Meanwhile, make the stuffing. Add a little olive oil to a large pot and sweat the shallots for 5 minutes. Add the chopped eggplant trimmings, garlic, and tomatoes. Allow to cook down for 15 minutes over a low heat.

Remove from the heat and mix in the parsley, chives, and piquillo peppers. Allow to cool.

Preheat the oven to 350°F/180°C/gas mark 4.

Rinse and dry the eggplant rounds, and brown them lightly in olive oil in a large skillet.

When the stuffing has cooled completely, stir in the pine nuts and ground lamb.

In an ovenproof dish, sauté the bacon pieces in a little olive oil, then add the onions and the cubes of green pepper. Cook for an additional 5–6 minutes, then add the water. Season, and add the thyme and the bay leaves. Remove from the heat.

Place a spoonful of stuffing in the hollow of each eggplant round and place on top of the vegetables in the dish. Cook for 30 minutes, uncovered, in the preheated oven.

Serve hot or cold.

Pan-fried chanterelles
with apricots and fresh almonds

2 tablespoons (1 oz./30 g) butter

1 lb. (500 g) chanterelles, cleaned

Salt and freshly ground black pepper

1 shallot, finely chopped

4 fresh apricots, diced

1 level teaspoon sugar

Scant ½ cup (3 ½ fl. oz./100 ml) white port

Bunch of chives, snipped

3 large white mushrooms

½ cup (3 oz./80 g) fresh almonds, shelled and skinned

Melt 1 tablespoon of butter in a skillet and sauté the chanterelles. Season with salt, then add the shallot.

Meanwhile, in a separate skillet, melt the remaining butter and sauté the apricots with the sugar.

When the chanterelles start to give off their water, add them, with their liquid, to the skillet with the apricots.

Allow to cook for several minutes, then add the port and cook for an additional 5 minutes. Check the seasoning, then stir in the chives.

Slice the large mushroom caps very finely on a mandoline.

Divide the chanterelle mixture and the fresh almonds between six serving bowls, sprinkle over the white mushroom slices, and serve.

Scallops marinière

Scant 1 cup (7 fl. oz./200 ml) lager beer

⅔ cup (5 fl. oz./150 ml) crème fraîche (or sour cream)

1 tablespoon mustard

½ cup (4 oz./120 g) cauliflower florets, cooked al dente

4 oz. (120 g) pear, diced (1 small pear)

10 oz. (280 g) scallops, diced

1 tablespoon snipped chives

Salt and pepper

Bring the beer to a boil in a cooking pot, add the crème fraîche, then the mustard, and whisk well until it comes back to a boil. Drop in the cauliflower and the diced pear, and bring back to a boil again.

Remove from the heat and add the scallops and chives. Stir carefully to combine.

Check the seasoning and serve in soup plates.

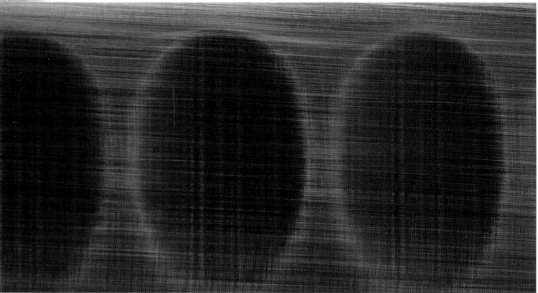

Smoked fish platter

9 oz. (250 g) fennel

1 tablespoon molasses

½ cup (4 fl. oz./125 ml) sheep's milk yogurt

Salt and freshly ground black pepper

4 oz. (120 g) smoked salmon

3 oz. (80 g) smoked eel

3 ½ oz. (100 g) smoked mackerel

Olive oil

Scant ½ cup (1 ½ oz./40 g) fresh red currants

1 ½ oz. (40 g) Manchego cheese, grated (⅓ cup grated)

Chop the fennel very finely and place in a bowl of ice water.

Mix the molasses with the sheep's milk yogurt and season with salt and pepper. Set aside in the refrigerator.

Arrange the smoked fish on four serving plates.

Drain and dry the fennel, put in a bowl and season with salt, pepper, and a dash of olive oil.

Stir in the red currants and the grated cheese. Place a spoonful in the center of each plate.

Serve the yogurt sauce on the side.

CHEF'S NOTE Manchego is a Spanish cheese from the region of La Mancha. Use a similar hard sheep's cheese if Manchego is unavailable, choosing the best quality available.

PREPARATION TIME: 15 MINUTES • COOKING TIME: 5 MINUTES • SERVES 4

Button mushroom,
salted plum, and shrimp wonton

1 cup (½ pint/250 ml) white wine

11 oz. (300 g) button mushrooms, cleaned

Salt and freshly ground white pepper

3 oz. (80 g) fresh bean sprouts, chopped

3 oz. (80 g) turnip, diced

2 oz. (50 g) salted plums, cut into ⅛ in. (3 mm) dice

11 oz. (300 g) shrimp tails, shelled

8 Chinese wonton wrappers

3 tablespoons olive oil

Bring the white wine to a boil, flambé it, then add the button mushrooms. Season lightly with salt, cover, and cook for a few minutes.

Remove from the heat and add the bean sprouts. Stir well, and allow to stand for 1–2 minutes. Set aside and, when the mixture has cooled, add the turnip, salted plums, and shrimp tails.

Cook the wonton wrappers in boiling salted water according to the package instructions, refresh in cold water, and drain. Set aside four whole wonton wrappers and cut the other four into strips.

Pour the broth into four soup plates, and add the strips of wonton. Top each soup plate with a whole wrapper and drizzle over a little olive oil before serving.

CHEF'S NOTE Salted plums can be found in Asian markets.

Crab, green mango,
pineapple, and green pepper salad

11 oz. (300 g) crabmeat

3 ½ oz. (100 g) pineapple, diced

2 ½ oz. (60 g) green mango, diced

Scant ½ cup (3 ½ oz./100 g) mustardy mayonnaise

3 ½ oz. (100 g) green bell pepper, sliced into strips

3 tablespoons oil

Salt and freshly ground white pepper

In a large bowl, stir together the crabmeat, pineapple, mango, and mayonnaise.

Arrange a large spoonful in the center of each of four individual serving plates.

Season the green pepper strips with olive oil, salt, and pepper. Arrange on top of the crab salad and serve.

Salad of fresh button mushrooms
with shiso leaves and salmon caviar

2 ½ oz. (60 g) salmon caviar

3 ½ oz. (100 g) lemon flesh, diced

11 oz. (320 g) button mushrooms, peeled and finely chopped

8 green shiso leaves

Salt and freshly ground white pepper

Toasted canola oil, to taste

Add a little water to the salmon caviar to loosen it and separate the eggs.

Combine the lemon flesh, mushrooms, and shiso leaves in a large mixing bowl. Season with salt, pepper, and a little canola oil.

Arrange in four salad bowls, and scatter over the salmon eggs. Serve immediately.

Zucchini, Parmesan,
and green olive salad with jellied Orvieto

1 cup (½ pint/250 ml) white wine (Orvieto)

3 gelatin leaves, soaked in cold water

1 medium zucchini, finely diced

⅓ cup (2 oz./50 g) pine nuts, toasted and chopped

¼ cup (2 oz./50 g) chopped green olives

3 ½ oz. (100 g) canned tuna in brine

3 tablespoons grated Parmesan

Lemon juice, to taste

Salt and freshly ground white pepper

Olive oil, to taste

Bring the white wine to a boil and flambé it. Add the soaked, drained gelatin leaves and stir until dissolved, then carefully pour into four soup bowls and set aside in a cool place to set.

In a large bowl, mix the zucchini, pine nuts, olives, and tuna. Add the Parmesan and season with a little lemon juice, salt, pepper, and olive oil.

Arrange this salad in the center of each wine jelly, and serve.

CHEF'S NOTE Orvieto is an off-dry white wine from Umbria.

Corn salad, cucumber, hazelnuts,
and Roquefort with Kirsch

For the cucumber with Kirsch:

Scant ½ cup (3 ½ fl. oz./100 ml) water

4 tablespoons sugar

4 ½ oz. (120 g) cucumber (½ small),
   peeled and diced

4 tablespoons Kirsch (cherry brandy)

For the salad:

¾ cup (4 oz./120 g) Muscatel grapes, halved

Hazelnut oil, to taste

Lemon juice, to taste

Salt and freshly ground white pepper

5 oz. (150 g) corn salad

¼ cup (1 ½ oz./40 g) hazelnuts, chopped

3 oz. (80 g) Roquefort cheese, crumbled

Prepare the cucumber with Kirsch a day ahead: bring the water and sugar to a boil, then allow to cool. Add the cucumber and Kirsch and leave in a cool place for 12 hours.

The next day, drain the cucumber, reserving the syrup. Put in a large mixing bowl with the grapes and drizzle over a little hazelnut oil, lemon juice, and Kirsch syrup, and season with salt and pepper.

Add the corn salad, toss to combine, and scatter over the hazelnuts and the Roquefort. Serve in a large salad bowl or four separate bowls.

VEGETABLES

PREPARATION TIME: 15 MINUTES · COOKING TIME: 10 MINUTES · SERVES 4

Cherry tomatoes with pastis

7 oz. (200 g) cherry tomatoes

2 tablespoons olive oil

Salt and freshly ground black pepper

3 tablespoons pastis

4 tablespoons liquid caramel

1 fennel bulb

Prick the cherry tomatoes with the point of a sharp knife. Heat the olive oil in a non-stick skillet and add the tomatoes. Season with salt, cover, lower the heat, and allow to cook down for 5 minutes.

Remove the lid, and turn up the heat. Pour over the pastis and the caramel and stir gently. Cook for 3–5 minutes.

Season generously with pepper.

Slice the fennel as finely as possible, using a mandoline, and divide the slices between four small plates.

Place the cherry tomatoes carefully on top of the fennel, and drizzle with the caramelized pan juices.

Potatoes, apples,
and blue cheese, flavored with cinnamon

14 oz. (400 g) apples (e.g. Clochard)

Mineral water

1 cup (½ pint/250 ml) long-life cream, heated

Pinch of cinnamon

1 lb. (500 g) new potatoes

Table salt and freshly ground white pepper

1 ½ oz. (30 g) blue cheese (e.g. Bleu des Causses), crumbled

Heat the oven to 350°F/180°C/gas mark 4.

Peel and core the apples and cut into chunks. Cook for 10 minutes in a cooking pot with a little mineral water. Purée using a stick blender. Add the hot cream a little at a time, then stir in the cinnamon.

Cook the potatoes, unpeeled, in a large pot of boiling, salted water. Drain and allow to cool a little before peeling and cutting into rounds.

Mix the applesauce and potatoes together and season.

Pour the mixture into a gratin dish and scatter over the blue cheese. Cook in the oven for 10–12 minutes.

Seaside tomatoes

6 ripe tomatoes

4 tablespoons olive oil

Salt and freshly ground black pepper

3 garlic cloves, finely chopped

Pinch dried thyme

1 dried bay leaf, crumbled

½ teaspoon sugar

2 ½ tablespoons (20 g) pine nuts, toasted

1 slice sandwich bread, in bread crumbs

2 sardines in oil, mashed

6 basil leaves, snipped (or 1 tablespoon frozen basil)

Arugula salad and balsamic vinegar, to serve

Heat the oven to 325°F/160°C/gas mark 3.

Wash the tomatoes, remove the stems, cut in half lengthwise and seed.

Oil an ovenproof serving dish. Sprinkle salt, pepper, garlic, thyme, and bay leaf over the bottom of the dish. Arrange the tomato halves over the top in tight rows, then sprinkle with sugar and a little more salt and pepper. Cook in the oven for 40 minutes.

When cooked, take out four cooked tomato halves, remove the skins, and roughly crush the flesh. Mix this purée with the pine nuts, bread crumbs, and mashed sardines. Check the seasoning and add the snipped basil.

Fill the remaining eight cooked tomato halves with this purée, and return to the oven for 5 minutes.

Serve the warm tomatoes with an arugula salad tossed with a spoonful of balsamic vinegar.

Pistoleto potatoes

½ teaspoon turmeric

½ teaspoon smoked paprika

1 tablespoon coriander seeds

Pinch of cumin seeds

Pinch of black peppercorns

½ teaspoon dried rosemary

1 teaspoon fleur de sel or kosher salt

1 ½ lb. (800 g) waxy potatoes (such as Charlotte)

Scant 1 cup (7 fl. oz./200 ml) sunflower oil

Crush the spices, rosemary, and salt in a small bowl, or with a mortar and pestle (or a spice grinder).

Peel the potatoes and cut them into large fries. Put them in a large pot of cold water and bring to a boil. When the water reaches boiling point, drain the potatoes, dry them, and rub them with the spice mixture.

Heat the sunflower oil in a wok. When the oil is hot, put the potatoes in and cook over a medium heat, turning regularly, until they are tender on the inside and crunchy on the outside.

CHEF'S NOTE Make sure the oil does not get too hot or you will burn the spices.

Tamy potatoes

2 lb. (1 kg) potatoes (Agria)

Kosher salt, table salt, and freshly ground white pepper

2 cups (9 oz./250 g) packaged bread crumbs

5 large medjool dates, finely diced

5 dried apricots, finely diced

5 dried figs, finely diced

5 oz. (150 g) Brillat-Savarin cheese, finely diced

Heat the oven to 400°F/200°C/gas mark 6.

Wash and dry the unpeeled potatoes. Scatter a thick layer of kosher salt in a shallow ovenproof dish and arrange the potatoes on top. Cook in the oven until they are tender in the middle when poked with a sharp knife (about 30–45 minutes, according to the size and age of the potatoes).

Remove the potatoes from the oven and split them in half. Scoop out the flesh and push it through a fine sieve or potato ricer while still hot. Season with salt and pepper.

Form the potato purée into 10 small patties 2 in. (5 cm) thick, and make an indentation in the top of each one. Dip in bread crumbs and set aside.

In a bowl, mix the dried fruits and cheese and place a spoonful in the hollow center of each patty.

Place in the oven for a few minutes, just long enough to melt the cheese.

CHEF'S NOTE Brillat-Savarin cheese is a round cow's milk cheese with bloomy white skin. It is creamy with a faintly sour, salty taste. You can substitute Brie if Brillat-Savarin is not available.

Lee's spinach salad

For the Lee sauce:

1 ¼ cups (10 fl. oz./300 ml) carrot juice

1 oz. (30 g) carrot, cut into ⅛ in./3 mm dice

Salt and pepper

Pinch of curry powder

1 tablespoon white balsamic vinegar

For the salad:

3 ½ oz. (100 g) baby spinach

3 tablespoons olive oil

Prepare the Lee sauce: bring the carrot juice to a boil in a small pot and reduce until there are only 3 tablespoons left.

Add the carrot dice to the reduced carrot juice. Season lightly with salt, and add the curry powder and white balsamic vinegar. Pour into a small glass container with a lid. Set aside for 12 hours in the refrigerator.

Wash and pick over the baby spinach and drain. Wrap in a clean damp cloth and set aside in the refrigerator.

Just before serving, pour 2 tablespoons of Lee sauce into a serving bowl, whisk in the olive oil, and season with pepper. Toss carefully with the baby spinach and serve immediately. The remaining sauce can be kept for 3–4 days in the refrigerator.

Braised endives and leeks
with truffles

2 endives

2 leeks, white parts only

1 tablespoon (½ oz./15 g) butter

Salt and freshly ground white pepper

Scant ½ cup (3 ½ fl. oz./100 ml) vegetable stock

2 tablespoons crème fraîche (or sour cream)

¾ oz. (20 g) truffles, shaved

Separate the endive leaves and cut them into julienne (⅛ in/3 mm) strips. Cut the white parts of the leeks to the same size. Heat the butter in a non-stick skillet, add the julienned vegetables and season lightly with salt. Sweat for 5 minutes over a medium heat, then add the vegetable stock. Allow to evaporate slightly, then add the crème fraîche and bring to a boil. Remove from the heat and sprinkle with the truffle shavings. Check the seasoning, and serve immediately in a warmed dish.

Pan-fried chestnuts

14 oz. (400 g) raw chestnuts

2 tablespoons (1 oz./30 g) butter

Salt and freshly ground white pepper

2 tablespoons white balsamic vinegar

1 ½ tablespoons grated aged Parmesan

First, peel the chestnuts: make a cross on the end of each one with a sharp knife and sauté them in a dry skillet over a high heat for 5 minutes. Remove from the heat and peel, making sure to remove the fluffy white inner skin as well. Roughly chop the chestnuts. Heat the butter in a non-stick skillet and add the chopped chestnuts. Cook for 6–7 minutes, and season lightly with salt. Pour the vinegar over the chestnuts and cook for a few minutes longer. Tip the chestnuts into a large, warmed serving bowl, grind over some black pepper, and sprinkle with grated Parmesan.

Jacquot's cauliflower

1 small cauliflower
Dash of vinegar
Scant 1 cup (7 fl. oz./200 ml) milk
Scant 1 cup (7 fl. oz./200 ml) pouring cream
1 oz. (30 g) Roquefort cheese, crumbled
3 ½ tablespoons (2 oz./50 g) butter
Freshly ground nutmeg
Salt and freshly ground white pepper
Juice of 1 lemon
6 savory tartlet shells
2 slices deli ham, diced

Remove the leaves from the cauliflower and clean it in water with a dash of vinegar added. Make a slit in the stem to aid cooking. Put in a large pot of boiling, salted water with the milk and cook for 25 minutes. Drain well, reserving the cooking liquid, taking care to keep the cauliflower in one piece.

Preheat the oven to 350°F/180°C/gas mark 4.

Return a cup of the cooking liquid to the pot, add the cream, and cook over a high heat for 5 minutes to reduce slightly. Add the crumbled Roquefort and allow to dissolve gently, then whisk vigorously, incorporating 2 tablespoons of butter and a grating of nutmeg.

Melt the remaining butter, season with salt and pepper and add the lemon juice. Pour the melted butter over the cauliflower.

Warm the tartlet shells for a few minutes in a warm oven. Arrange the pieces of ham in the bottom of each tartlet and place on individual serving plates.

Serve the cauliflower whole, allowing guests to serve themselves by adding a large spoonful of cauliflower to their tartlet.

Coco

1 banana

1 oz. (30 g) coconut flesh

½ green bell pepper

7 oz. (200 g) bean sprouts

Salt and pepper

Zest of 1 organic lemon

1 tablespoon maple syrup

2 ½ tablespoons golden raisins, soaked in a little water

Scant ½ cup (3 ½ fl. oz./100 ml) coconut cream

Scant ½ cup (3 ½ fl. oz./100 ml) light cream

4 egg yolks

Heat the oven to 400°F/200°C/gas mark 6.

Slice the banana thinly, place on a tray covered with plastic wrap, and freeze.

Shave the coconut flesh using a potato peeler.

Place the green bell pepper in the oven until the skin begins to blister. Remove and put into a plastic bag and allow to cool for a few minutes. The skin will then peel off easily. Seed and cut into ⅛ in. (3 mm) dice.

Cut the bean sprouts into small batons and steam for 3 minutes. Season with salt and add the lemon zest and the maple syrup. Mix with the golden raisins and diced pepper and transfer to a shallow ovenproof dish.

Put the coconut cream and light cream into a cooking pot and bring to a boil. Remove from the heat, whisk in the egg yolks, season, and pour over the vegetables. Cook in the oven for 4–5 minutes.

Remove from the oven and sprinkle with the fresh coconut and the frozen banana slices. Serve immediately.

Stiletto eggplants

2 eggplants
Salt and freshly ground black pepper
1 onion, diced
5 garlic cloves
1 cup (½ pint/250 ml) olive oil
1 medium tomato, diced
3 ¼ tablespoons honey
⅓ cup (2 ½ fl. oz./70 ml) sherry vinegar

Cut the eggplants into 1 in. (2.5 cm) thick slices and salt both sides. Leave for about 1 hour to draw out the moisture.

Cook the onion and the garlic in the olive oil for 3 minutes. Add the diced tomato, honey, and sherry vinegar. Allow to simmer for 30 minutes.

Sauté the eggplant slices in olive oil until golden. Stack the eggplant slices in a glass jar, alternating eggplant and tomato sauce. Store at the bottom of the refrigerator and use within 4–5 days.

FISH

PREPARATION TIME: 15 MINUTES · MARINATING TIME: 1 HOUR
COOKING TIME: 15 MINUTES · SERVES 6

Salmon with acacia honey

6 organic salmon fillets (3 ½ oz./100 g pieces
  cut from the back fillet)

1 tablespoon liquid honey (acacia)

2 dill sprigs, snipped

Zest and juice of 1 organic lime

1 tablespoon green peppercorns, crushed

3 ½ oz. (100 g) black radish

1 handful baby spinach

5 sorrel leaves

2 tablespoons Fjord® yogurt, or sour cream

1 tablespoon oil

Salt and freshly ground white pepper

Arrange the salmon fillets in a shallow dish. Warm the honey, and stir in the snipped dill, lime zest, and crushed green peppercorns. Pour this marinade over the salmon portions. Cover with plastic wrap and allow to marinate for 1 hour.

Cut the black radish into julienne (⅛ in./3 mm) sticks. Pick over the baby spinach. Chop the sorrel leaves. Mix the yogurt with a drizzle of olive oil, and season with salt and pepper.

Heat a non-stick skillet with a drop of olive oil. Remove the salmon portions from the marinade, add to the skillet, season, and cook over a medium heat for 8 minutes. Pour over the remaining marinade, cover, and allow to cook for an additional 3 minutes. Remove from the heat, and allow to rest for 1 minute to finish cooking.

In a salad bowl, toss together the sorrel, black radish, and baby spinach with the yogurt dressing and a splash of lime juice. Arrange between six individual bowls, and place a salmon portion on each one.

CHEF'S NOTE Fjord® yogurt is a slightly sour, unsweetened brand of yogurt. Substitute sour cream or European-style unsweetened yogurt.

Codfish broth

1 hard-boiled egg yolk

1 tablespoon wasabi

1 tablespoon miso

Salt

1 ¼ lb. (600 g) skinless cod fillet

½ pear

2 oz. (50 g) black radish

2 sheets nori seaweed

4 cups (2 pints/900 ml) Leek broth with seaweed
and bonito flakes (see page 93)

6 juniper berries

Pass the egg yolk through a fine sieve. Mix with the wasabi and miso to form a thick paste and season with a little salt. Roll into six walnut-sized balls and set aside in the refrigerator, covered with plastic wrap.

Cut the cod into large chunks, season with salt, and set aside on a small plate in the refrigerator.

Peel and core the pear, peel the black radish, and cut both into small dice. Cut the nori sheets into thin strips and set aside.

Bring the broth to a boil.

Arrange the chunks of cod, pear, black radish, and one juniper berry in six individual soup bowls, and pour over the boiling broth. Cover each bowl with plastic wrap and allow to rest for 5 minutes to cook the fish.

To serve, place the strips of nori and the little balls of wasabi egg yolk on top of the plastic wrap. Each guest pierces their plastic wrap, allowing the nori and wasabi to fall into the broth and flavor it.

CHEF'S NOTE Miso is a traditional Japanese ingredient, a fermented paste that has a very pronounced flavor (white miso is less strong; dark brown is the strongest in taste). Miso is often made from soy and sometimes rice or barley.

Sea bream granita
with lime, white rum, and coconut water

2 x 11 oz. (300 g) skinless sea bream fillets

Zest and juice of 1 organic lime

Scant ½ cup (3 ½ fl. oz./100 ml) coconut water

1 tablespoon white rum

1 tablespoon pink peppercorns

Salt and freshly ground white pepper

1 green mango

1 cup (125 g) Fjord® yogurt, or sour cream

Cut the sea bream fillets into small evenly sized cubes and place in a bowl. Add the lime zest and juice, coconut water, white rum, and pink peppercorns. Season, toss gently, and place in the freezer for 2 hours. Mix regularly so that the mixture takes on the texture of a granita.

Peel and pit the mango and cut the flesh into ⅛ in. (3 mm) dice.

Spread the yogurt over individual plates, arrange a spoonful of fish granita on top and sprinkle with diced mango. Season with pepper.

Serve immediately with toasted country-style bread.

CHEF'S NOTE You can find coconut water in Asian markets (canned or frozen).

Fjord® yogurt is a slightly sour, unsweetened brand of yogurt. Substitute sour cream or European-style unsweetened yogurt.

"Clos des loups" cod fillet

1 cup (7 oz./200 g) medium-grain couscous

3 tablespoons olive oil

½ teaspoon *ras el hanout*

Salt

2 cups (1 pint/500 ml) Vegetable infusion
(see page 95)

2 lemon balm sprigs

2 fresh cilantro sprigs

4 x 3 ½ oz. (100 g) thick cod steaks

3 ½ oz. (100 g) green bell pepper, diced

3 ½ oz. (100 g) fresh pineapple flesh, diced

⅓ cup (2 oz./50 g) dried apricots, quartered

Pour the couscous into a large bowl and stir in a tablespoon of olive oil, the *ras el hanout*, and half a teaspoon of salt. Heat a cupful of vegetable infusion to boiling point and pour it over the couscous. Cover the bowl and allow the couscous to swell for 10 minutes.

Heat the oven to 400°F/200°C/gas mark 6.

In the bowl of a food processor, mix the lemon balm and cilantro with the remaining olive oil and a pinch of salt to make a paste. Brush this mixture over the four cod portions, place them on a plate, cover with plastic wrap, and set aside in the refrigerator.

Fork through the couscous to fluff up the grains, then stir in the diced pepper, pineapple, and apricots.

Arrange four large sheets of aluminum foil on a baking sheet. Drop a large spoonful of fruity couscous on the center of each sheet, and top each with a piece of cod. Pour 4 tablespoons of Vegetable infusion over each one and fold up the foil to make little packets.

Place in the oven and cook for 8 minutes. Remove from the oven and serve, allowing guests to open their own packet at the table.

CHEF'S NOTE *Ras el hanout* is a North African blend of spices that may contain up to 30 different ingredients. If you can't find it, you may substitute a pinch of curry powder.

Oysters in a tangy broth

1 tablespoon cider vinegar
Salt and freshly ground white pepper
3 tablespoons sunflower oil
Splash of toasted sesame oil
2 slices of sandwich bread
6 oysters, size 2

1 sour herring fillet, or rollmop, about 2 oz. (50 g)
3 ½ oz. (100 g) endive, cut into ⅛ in. (3 mm) batons
1 ½ oz. (40 g) radicchio, cut into ⅛ in. (3 mm) batons
3 cups (1 ½ pints/750 ml) Leek broth with seaweed and bonito flakes (see page 93)

Pour the cider vinegar into a small bowl and season with salt and pepper. Whisk in 2 tablespoons of sunflower oil and the sesame oil.

Cut the crusts off the bread and cut into small cubes.

Heat the remaining sunflower oil in a non-stick skillet. When the oil is hot, fry the bread cubes until golden, then drain on paper towels.

Open the oysters, remove from their shells, and drain. Cut the herring into small dice.

Place the batons of endive and radicchio in a large bowl and pour over the vinaigrette. Arrange small piles of salad in individual serving bowls.

Top each salad with a raw oyster, sprinkle with diced herring, then pour over a little cold broth.

Serve the croutons separately, so guests may help themselves at the table.

CHEF'S NOTE Radicchio was originally a wild leaf chicory that originated in Venetia. It grows as a little clump of dark-red, round-tipped leaves veined with white. It is bitter in taste and should be crisp in texture. When it is out of season, you can use chicory leaves.

The bitterness of the leaves can be used in unexpectedly delicious ways—a mixture of radicchio, beet, and tamarillo, for example.

Scallops grilled on the half-shell

4 large scallops (see Chef's note)

½ teaspoon Madras curry powder

Pinch of dehydrated orange powder
(available online)

Fleur de sel

3 sprigs flat-leaf parsley, crushed

7 oz. (200 g) black radish

1 cup (½ pint/250 ml) Leek broth with seaweed
and bonito flakes (see page 93)

2 tablespoons soy sauce

Pinch of sugar

Salt and freshly ground white pepper

Butter

Peel the black radish and cut it into four large slices. Place the slices in a small pot with the broth, soy sauce, and sugar, season, and allow to simmer for 20 minutes until the radish is cooked through. Drain and set aside.

Heat the oven to 350°F/180°C/gas mark 4.

Heat a tablespoon of butter in a non-stick skillet and cook the scallops, flesh-side down, for 3 minutes. Remove from the skillet and place them shell-side down on a baking sheet. Place in the oven and cook for 6–8 minutes.

Add another small piece of butter to the skillet and sauté the braised black radish slices briefly.

Take the scallops from the oven and arrange on warmed plates. Top each one with a slice of radish.

Mix the curry powder and the orange powder with a pinch of fleur de sel. Add another small piece of butter to the skillet. When it is foamy, add this spice mix and the parsley. Pour this sauce over the scallops and serve immediately.

CHEF'S NOTE Ask your fishmonger to open the scallops for you, leaving the scallop still attached to the upper shell.

Grilled sea bass

6 x 4 oz. (120 g) sea bass fillets, scales left on

Scant 1 cup (7 fl. oz./200 ml) peanut oil, heated

3 tablespoons (1 ½ oz./40 g) butter

Salt and freshly ground white pepper

7 oz. (200 g) samphire

2 oz. (50 g) dulse flakes

3 ½ oz. (100 g) cuttlefish, or squid, diced

11 oz. (300 g) Brussels sprouts

Preheat the oven to 325°F/160°C/gas mark 3.

Place the sea bass fillets on a broiler pan, skin-side up, and pour over the hot peanut oil. The scales will stick up a little. Allow to rest for 1 minute, then place the sea bass fillets in a shallow dish and dot with butter. Season with salt and pepper and cook in the oven for 8 minutes, basting frequently.

When cooked, remove from the oven, transfer to a serving dish, and keep warm.

Cook the samphire for 3 minutes in boiling, salted water, and drain. Mix with the dulse flakes and diced cuttlefish or squid. Season and add a little melted butter to bind. Set aside in a warm place.

Trim the Brussels sprouts and cut into quarters. Cook for 5 minutes in boiling, salted water until al dente. Drain, then refresh under cold water.

Melt a little butter in a large pot and add the drained sprouts. Season with salt and pepper and cook over a low heat for 5 minutes. Arrange the sprouts in individual plates, top with a sea bass fillet, and sprinkle with the samphire–dulse–cuttlefish mixture. Serve immediately.

CHEF'S NOTE Dulse is an edible seaweed, reddish or even purple, with a light, slightly briny taste. Samphire, also known as sea fennel, grows in coastal areas. It has fleshy, edible stems.

Sole goujons with colombo spices

1 cup (7 oz./200 g) couscous

3 tablespoons olive oil

Salt and freshly ground white pepper

Scant 1 cup (7 fl. oz./200 ml) mineral water

6 x 7 oz. (200 g) sole fillets, prepared
  by your fishmonger

7 oz. (200 g) brown button mushrooms

2 tablespoons (1 oz./30 g) butter

½ teaspoon colombo powder

Scant ½ cup (3 ½ fl. oz./100 ml) white port

2 cups (1 pint/500 ml) champagne

2 oz. (50 g) croutons

Mix the couscous with 2 tablespoons of the olive oil and season lightly with salt. Bring the mineral water to a boil, pour it over the couscous, and allow to swell.

Cut the sole fillets into small goujons 1 ¼ in. (3 cm) long.

Chop the mushrooms finely and sauté them in the remaining olive oil until they are lightly caramelized.

Heat 2 tablespoons of butter in a non-stick skillet and add the colombo. Cook for 2 minutes over a low heat to release the flavor of the spices.

Add the sole goujons and cook for 5–6 minutes over a medium heat, spooning over the butter regularly. When almost cooked, add 3 tablespoons of water and mix with the butter to make a sauce.

Heat the port and champagne gently in a pot then pour it over the couscous and mix well. Divide the couscous between six warmed bowls, arrange the goujons of sole over the top, and pour over the cooking liquid. Sprinkle with the sautéed mushrooms and the croutons.

CHEF'S NOTE Colombo is the Caribbean equivalent of curry powder, and like curry powder, it is not a spice but a mixture of spices that make up a yellow-hued powder. It was probably introduced to the Caribbean by Indian workers from 1862 onward. Colombo contains turmeric, cumin, coriander, cloves, black pepper, fenugreek, mustard, ginger, and, in some cases, ground rice. The addition of ground rice adds a binding property that can be useful when making sauces.

Poached brill
with pink radish, egg, and grr... sauce

1 ear of corn	**For the grr... sauce:**
10 pink radishes	3 hard-boiled eggs, chopped
2 tablespoons (1 oz./30 g) butter	½ cup (2 oz./50 g) red currants
6 x 3 ½ oz. (100 g) brill fillets	¼ green bell pepper, cut into ⅛ in. (3 mm) dice
Salt and freshly ground black pepper	2 scallions, finely chopped
	1 tablespoon snipped chives
	1 tablespoon *achards de citron* (candied spiced lemon, available online)
	1 tablespoon rice vinegar
	1 birds-eye chili, crushed
	2 tablespoons (1 oz./30 g) butter, melted

First make the grr... sauce: place the hard-boiled eggs, red currants, bell pepper, scallion, chives, *achard de citron*, rice vinegar, birds-eye chili, and melted butter in a bowl and stir to combine.

Grate the fresh corn and the radishes on a mandoline, steam them briefly, and set aside.

Preheat the oven to 350°F/180°C/gas mark 4.

Heat a tablespoon of the butter in a non-stick skillet and sauté the brill fillets briefly, then place in the oven for about 6 minutes to finish cooking. When just cooked through, remove from the oven and remove the skin. Arrange on a warmed plate.

Heat the remaining tablespoon of butter in the skillet and, when it is foamy and starts to turn brown, add the sauce, and any juice given off by the fish during cooking. Season well and pour over the fish fillets to serve.

Pollack shavings
on a bed of apples with calvados

2 eggs

1 cup (½ pint/250 ml) light cream

Salt and freshly ground white pepper and nutmeg

2 apples (Reinettes)

Butter, for greasing the dish

Dash of calvados

¼ cup (1 ½ oz./40 g) grated Parmesan cheese

6 x 2 oz. (50 g) pollack fillets

Small piece of Montpellier butter (see page 197)

Preheat the oven to 350°F/180°C/gas mark 4.

Whisk the eggs and the cream together. Season with salt, pepper, and nutmeg.

Peel and core the apples and cut them in half and then into thin slices. Spread out the apple slices in a buttered ovenproof dish. Pour over a little calvados, then the egg and cream mixture. Sprinkle over the grated Parmesan and cook in the oven for 20 minutes.

Meanwhile, cut the pollack fillets into fine slices. Oil a circle of parchment paper, and arrange the slices of pollack on it. Season with salt and pepper.

When the apple gratin is cooked, flip the circle of paper onto the top of the gratin, paper-side up, then remove the paper. Dot with some Montpellier butter. Return to the oven for a few minutes, so that the fish is just cooked through; it should just be pearly white. Serve immediately.

MEAT

PREPARATION TIME: 35 MINUTES · MARINATING TIME: 24 HOURS
COOKING TIME: 10 MINUTES · SERVES 6

Beef and sardine gonzo

½ cup (3 ½ oz./100 g) muscovado sugar
(brown sugar may be substituted)

3 tablespoons rice vinegar

1 cup (½ pint/250 ml) orange juice, heated

2 tablespoons mirin

3 tablespoons soy sauce

3 tablespoons olive oil

11 oz. (300 g) beef tenderloin

2 beefheart tomatoes

Salt and freshly ground pepper

⅓ cup (2 oz./50 g) chickpea flour

12 Mediterranean sardine fillets

1 green Zebra tomato

Yuzu juice, or lime juice, to taste

1 red onion, cut into wedges

Pinch of sugar

1 cup (2 oz./50 g) flat-leaf parsley

½ cup (¾ oz./20 g) cilantro leaves

A day ahead, put the sugar in a cooking pot and heat gently to dissolve. Add the rice vinegar, hot orange juice, mirin, and soy sauce. Cook until you have a light caramel.

In a lightly oiled skillet, sear the beef over a high heat to color the exterior. Place it in a shallow dish, pour over half the caramel, and allow to marinate for 24 hours. Set aside the remaining caramel. Cut six ½ in. (1 cm) thick slices from the beefheart tomatoes. Season with salt and pepper and coat with chickpea flour. Sauté in a skillet with the remaining oil until golden, then set aside to keep warm.

Sauté the sardines, skin-side down, then place in a shallow dish. In the same skillet, heat the remaining caramel. Pour over the sardines and set aside. Cut the green tomato into small dice and season with salt, pepper, and a dash of yuzu juice.

In the skillet, sauté the onion and add a little sugar. Season with salt, pepper, and a dash of yuzu juice. Drain the beef from its marinade and slice finely. Sprinkle with a little marinade and pepper. Finely chop the parsley and cilantro and season with a little of the marinade.

Arrange the salad on six plates: start with the red onions, then add the tomato slices, sardines, green tomato, beef, and finish with the parsley–cilantro salad.

CHEF'S NOTE Muscovado is a brown unrefined cane sugar, available from specialty suppliers. It is also known as Barbados sugar.

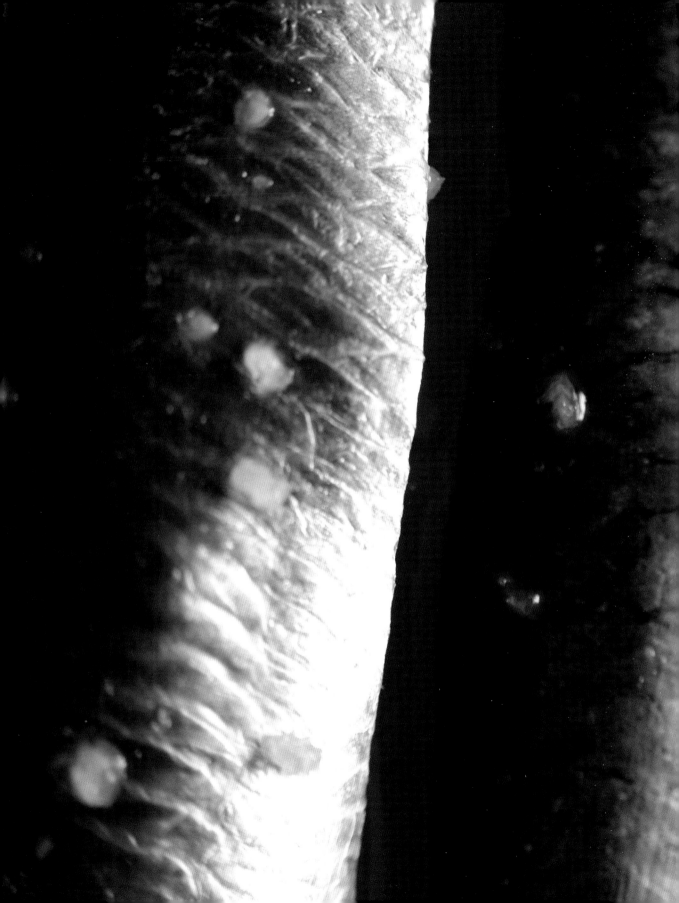

Rolled beef in aniseed broth

1 onion

Small piece of fresh ginger (about 1 oz./30 g)

1 lb. (500 g) black radish

2 carrots

2 celery sticks

4 ¼ cups (2 pints/1 liter) mineral water

¼ stock cube

1 star anise

1 cinnamon stick

2 cloves

1 lb. (500 g) beef tenderloin, tied into a roast

Fleur de sel and freshly ground black pepper

Peel the onion and ginger and cut the onion in half. Heat a non-stick skillet, with no fat. Cook the halved onion and ginger in the skillet for 10 minutes over a medium heat. The surfaces should be blackened.

Peel the vegetables, then cut the black radish and carrots into 1 in. (2.5 cm) thick slices and the celery into small sticks.

Heat the water with the stock cube and add the blackened ginger and onion, the star anise, cinnamon, and cloves. Bring to a boil and skim off any impurities that rise to the surface. Add the vegetables and simmer for 30 minutes. When the vegetables are cooked, remove the onion and ginger.

Put the beef joint in the boiling broth and cook for 10–15 minutes (10–15 minutes per pound/500 g). It should still be pink in the center when done.

Remove the beef from the broth, take off the string, and cut into thick slices.

Arrange the vegetables between four soup bowls, pour over a little broth, and top with a slice of beef. Sprinkle with salt and pepper.

Serve with relishes and sauces on the side (Sauces and Condiments, pages 186–9).

CHEF'S NOTE A tip to keep your fleur de sel or kosher salt crunchy even when it gets damp: mix it with a little olive oil before using.

Surf and turf tartare

1 lb. (500 g) beef tenderloin
7 oz. (200 g) sea bream fillet
3 ½ oz. (100 g) herring
1 gherkin
2 tablespoons water
2 tablespoons olive oil
1 teaspoon Worcestershire sauce
Dash of Tabasco
1 teaspoon capers, chopped
½ tablespoon finely chopped shallot
Salt and freshly ground black pepper
Crisp green pears, to serve

Cut the beef tenderloin, sea bream, and herring into small cubes. Set aside, in separate dishes, in the refrigerator. Cut the gherkin into ⅛ in. (3 mm) dice.

To make the dressing, in a large bowl, whisk the water and olive oil with the Worcestershire sauce and Tabasco.

Add the meat, fish, gherkin, capers, and shallot and stir to combine. Check the seasoning.

Arrange on cold plates and serve with quarters of crisp green pear.

Grilled sausages
with corn and maple syrup

3 ½ oz (100 g) evenly sized Charlotte potatoes
1 tablespoon sunflower oil
2 Toulouse sausages, or sweet Italian sausages
½ teaspoon black pepper
2 tablespoons sherry vinegar
Scant ½ cup (3 ½ fl. oz./100 ml) maple syrup
2 cooked ears of corn, kernels removed with sharp knife

Cook the potatoes in their skins in a pot of boiling water.

Meanwhile, heat the oil in a non-stick skillet, and cook the sausages. Remove from the pan and cut into slices.

Return the sausage to the skillet, season with pepper, and deglaze with the vinegar. Stir in the maple syrup and corn kernels and cook for an additional 4–5 minutes.

Serve with the potatoes.

Pepper steak

2 tablespoons sunflower oil

1 lb. (500 g) skirt steak

Salt

3 ½ tablespoons (2 oz./50 g) butter

1 teaspoon black sesame seeds

2 tablespoons mixed peppercorns, crushed

2 tablespoons cognac

3 tablespoons crème fraîche (or sour cream)

½ stock cube

Add a little sunflower oil to a skillet and, when it is very hot, sear the steak briefly on one side. Season with salt then turn over and cook the other side. Cook until the steak is still rare, then set aside on a plate.

Add the butter, sesame seeds, and crushed pepper to the same skillet and cook for 5 minutes. Return the steak to the pan, basting it with the peppery butter. Remove the steak and buttery juices to a dish and keep warm.

Pour the cognac into the skillet and stir in the crème fraîche and crumbled stock cube. Reduce for 3 minutes over a high heat.

Slice the meat, pour the sauce over, and serve immediately with thick fries.

Grilled lamb chops
with Arty eggplants

12 lamb chops

1 tablespoon olive oil

Pinch of cinnamon

Sprigs of herbs such as thyme, rosemary, and summer savory

Salt and freshly ground black pepper

For the Arty eggplants:

11 oz. (300 g) eggplants, diced

Salt and freshly ground black pepper

2 tablespoons olive oil

½ cup (4 fl. oz./120 ml) red wine (Syrah)

Scant ½ cup (3 ½ fl. oz./100 ml) port

½ cup (2 ½ oz./70 g) dried apricots, diced

½ cup (2 ½ oz./70 g) fresh figs, diced

First make the Arty eggplants: preheat the oven to 350°F/180°C/gas mark 4. Sprinkle the diced eggplant with salt and set aside for 20 minutes to draw out the moisture.

Squeeze to remove any excess liquid, then sauté briefly in a skillet with a little olive oil, until lightly colored.

Bring the wine and the port to a boil in a large cooking pot, and flambé (to remove the alcohol). Add the diced fruit and the sautéed eggplant and season with salt and pepper. Cover with a piece of parchment paper, place in the oven, and cook for 25 minutes.

Brush the lamb chops with a little olive oil. Sprinkle over the cinnamon and herbs and season with salt and pepper. Cover with plastic wrap and set aside at room temperature until ready to cook.

Grill the lamb chops on a barbecue or cook them, without oil, in a very hot non-stick skillet. When the eggplant is cooked, remove from the oven and take off the paper.

Place the cooked lamb chops on top and return to the oven for 5 minutes.

Serve immediately.

Milk-fed lamb
with new potatoes and prunes

2 garlic cloves

1 teaspoon ground cumin

1 teaspoon dried mint

1 leg of milk-fed lamb, partially deboned,
   (aitch bone removed)

Kosher salt

3 onions

14 oz. (400 g) new potatoes
   (Ratte, if possible)

8 prunes, pitted

Thyme sprigs and bay leaves

3 large purple shallots, halved

2 tablespoons olive oil

Butter

Salt and freshly ground pepper

1 ¼ cups (10 fl. oz./300 ml) Jurançon wine
   (semi-sweet white wine)

Crush one garlic clove and mix with the cumin and the mint. Rub the leg of lamb with this mixture and kosher salt and place in a large dish. Cover with plastic wrap and leave for 20 minutes.

Peel the onions and potatoes and chop them into fine rounds.

Preheat the oven to 425°F/220°C/gas mark 7.

Cut the remaining garlic clove in half and rub the inside of a large ovenproof dish. Spread the onions, then the potatoes, in fine layers in the dish, scatter with prunes, and stick in a little thyme and a bay leaf here and there. Place the leg of lamb and the shallots on top, drizzle with a little olive oil, add a few knobs of butter, and season. Place in the oven and cook for 15 minutes until the lamb starts to color.

Pour over the wine, turn down the oven to 350°F/180°C/gas mark 4, and cook for an additional 20 minutes, or longer if you like your lamb less rare.

Serve in the ovenproof dish. The onions and potatoes will be deliciously cooked in the meat juices.

CHEF'S NOTE In season, replace the prunes with plums, Mirabelles, damsons, or peaches.

Devilled grilled poussins

¼ cup (1 oz./30 g) pale bread crumbs

¼ cup (¾ oz./20 g) ground hazelnuts

Salt and freshly ground black pepper

2 poussins, 1–1 ½ lb. (600–700g) each,
   cut in half and flattened

3 tablespoons mustard

4 tablespoons sunflower oil

12 cherry tomatoes

8 thin slices of smoked bacon

For the sauce diable:

Scant ½ cup (3 ½ fl. oz./100 ml) dry white wine

2 shallots, finely chopped

Salt and freshly ground black pepper

1 tablespoon Worcestershire sauce

2 tablespoons ketchup

3 dashes of Tabasco

1 tablespoon olive oil

1 tablespoon snipped tarragon

Preheat the oven to 400°F/200°C/gas mark 6.

Combine the bread crumbs and the ground hazelnuts. Season the poussins, brush the skin sides with mustard and sprinkle with the bread crumb mixture. Place in an ovenproof dish, skin-side up, drizzle with the sunflower oil and place in the oven. Cook for 20 minutes.

Meanwhile, make the sauce. Pour the wine into a cooking pot and add the chopped shallots and some freshly ground black pepper. Cook until almost evaporated, then add a glass of water, the Worcestershire sauce, ketchup, Tabasco, and olive oil, and continue to cook to mix all the flavors. Season, and finish with the snipped tarragon. Keep warm until ready to use.

When the poussins are almost cooked through and the bread crumbs are golden brown, turn the oven temperature down to 350°F/180°C/gas mark 4 and add the cherry tomatoes and the slices of bacon to the dish. Cook for an additional 10 minutes.

Remove the poussins from the oven and arrange on a shallow dish, surrounded by the tomatoes and bacon. Serve the sauce separately.

Free-range chicken and squid
with green curry sauce and white rum

2 chicken breasts

3 ½ oz. (100 g) cuttlefish, or squid

3 tablespoons sunflower oil

1 shallot, finely chopped

2 lemongrass sticks, snipped

3 garlic cloves, minced

1 tablespoon Thai green curry paste

1 ¼ cups (10 fl. oz./300 ml) coconut cream,
  or coconut milk

Scant ½ cup (3 ½ fl. oz./100 ml) heavy cream

Juice of 1 lime

2 tablespoons Caribbean white rum

1 tablespoon brown sugar

1 small green bell pepper, seeded and diced

2 fresh cilantro sprigs

Salt

Cut the chicken breasts into thin strips and dice the cuttlefish or squid.

Heat the oil in a large pot, and add the shallot, lemongrass, and garlic. Sweat for 5 minutes over a low heat then add the curry paste and cook for an additional 5 minutes. The oil will turn green.

Pour in the coconut cream a little at a time, cooking to reduce by half each time.

Add the chicken pieces and the heavy cream, and cook for an additional 15 minutes over a low heat.

When the chicken is cooked through, add the lime juice, rum, and brown sugar. Check the seasoning and bring back to a boil. Just before serving, add the diced green bell pepper and the squid to the curry sauce and stir gently to combine.

Sprinkle with fresh cilantro and serve hot with white rice.

CHEF'S NOTE Thai green curry paste can be found in Asian stores or in the Asian aisle of the supermarket, canned or in packet form. It is a wet curry paste, a mixture of ingredients that would originally have been crushed together in a mortar and pestle. It includes, among other things, galangal, fermented shrimp paste, green bell peppers, kaffir lime leaves, shallots, and coriander root.

SAUCES AND CONDIMENTS

PREPARATION TIME: 25 MINUTES · COOKING TIME: 1 ¼ HOURS · MAKES ABOUT 10 ½ OZ. (300 G)

Grandma's tomato sauce

1 lb. (500 g) tomatoes
1 cup (7 oz./200 g) brown sugar
5 garlic cloves
1 tablespoon fresh rosemary leaves
⅓ cup (3 fl. oz./80 ml) sherry vinegar
Salt and freshly ground black pepper

Preheat the oven to 300°F/150°C/gas mark 2.

Chop the tomatoes in half and seed them. Put the seeds in a fine sieve and push down to extract the juice.

Place the sugar in a griddle pan or baking sheet with sides and caramelize over a medium heat. Place the tomatoes skin-side up on top of the caramel, add the garlic and scatter over the rosemary. Pour over the vinegar and the tomato juice from the seeds.

Place in the oven and roast for about 1 ¼ hours until the tomatoes are lightly colored. Take out of the oven and remove the tomato skins as well as the rosemary and the garlic.

Process the tomatoes in a food processor, adding some of the cooking liquid if necessary to reach the desired consistency. Season to taste.

TTB sauce

7 oz. (200 g) tamarillos
12 oz. (350 g) Grandma's tomato sauce (see page 186)
9 oz. (250 g) cooked beets
Salt and freshly ground black pepper

Peel the tamarillos with a vegetable peeler. Cut the fruit in two and put them in a pan with a small amount of water. Cover, bring to a boil, and simmer for 15 minutes until very soft with a texture like purée.

In a food processor, mix all the ingredients together to make a smooth, red paste. Check the seasoning, and pass through a sieve.

CHEF'S NOTE The tamarillo is a small egg-shaped fruit about 2–4 in. (5–10 cm) in length. Its smooth, bitter skin is not edible and its flesh is firm and slightly acidic. There are two main commercially available varieties of tamarillo; one is a golden orange color with yellowish flesh, and the other has dark purple skin and orange flesh. It is better to use the latter in this recipe.

Crunchy sauce

3 ½ tablespoons (2 oz./50 g) butter

11 oz. (300 g) yellow bell peppers, peeled (see method on page 157) and diced

14 oz. (400 g) pears, peeled and diced

7 oz. (200 g) tomatoes, diced

11 oz. (300 g) grapefruit flesh, chopped

Salt and freshly ground white pepper

In a wide cooking pot, melt the butter and sweat the diced yellow bell pepper without allowing it to color. Season lightly with salt.

Add the diced pears and tomatoes and cook for 10–15 minutes.

Add the grapefruit flesh and cook over a medium heat, uncovered, stirring from time to time, until the liquid has evaporated and the mixture is thick.

Check the seasoning, and serve hot or cold.

Mustard paste

2 hard-boiled egg yolks

1 ½ oz. (40 g) turnip, very finely chopped

1 ½ tablespoons hazelnut oil

4 pinches of Colman's mustard powder

4 pinches of dehydrated orange powder (available online)

Lemon juice, to taste

Salt and freshly ground white pepper

Push the hard-boiled egg yolks through a sieve into a bowl. Add the turnip, hazelnut oil, mustard powder, and dehydrated orange powder and mix together to make a smooth paste. Season to taste with lemon juice, salt, and pepper.

Refrigerate for 1 hour before serving. The paste can be kept in the refrigerator for up to a week.

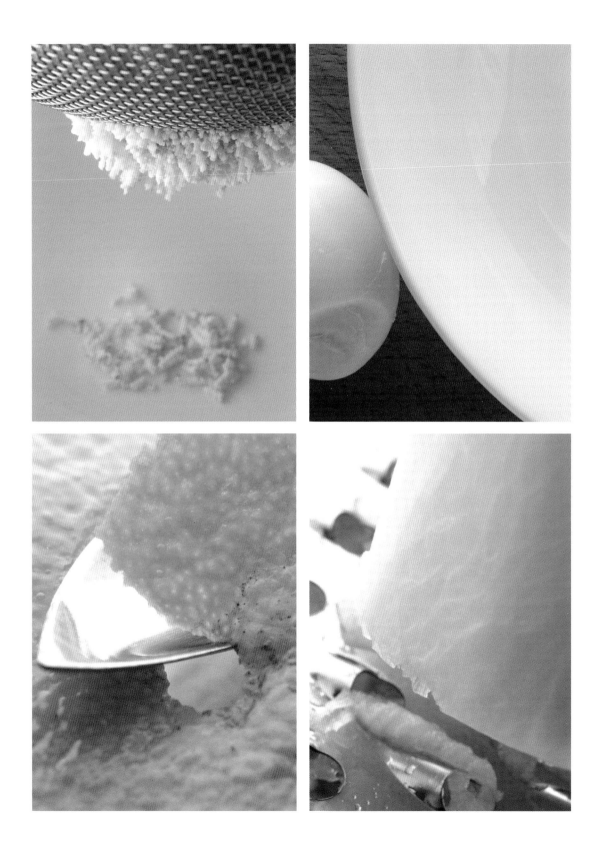

Red onion coulis
with tamarind

2 tablespoons olive oil
1 lb. (450 g) red onions, finely chopped
Salt and freshly ground black pepper
¼ cup (2 oz./60 g) tamarind paste

Put the olive oil and onions in a large cooking pot, season with salt, and cook over a low heat, uncovered, until the onions are softened. Add a little water if necessary.

In the bowl of a food processor, mix the hot cooked onions with the tamarind paste until well combined. Check the seasoning.

Remove from the heat and keep in a cool place until needed.

Watercress butter

4 oz. (120 g) watercress leaves
2 sticks (9 oz./250 g) salted butter, at room temperature

Chop the watercress leaves in a food processor and add the butter a little at a time. Wrap the green butter in plastic wrap and roll into a stick shape. Keep in the refrigerator.

Coë sauce

Scant ½ cup (3 oz./80 g) sugar

3 oz. (80 g) onion, very finely chopped

3 ½ tablespoons soy sauce

3 ½ tablespoons rice wine vinegar

2 garlic cloves, very finely chopped

1 tablespoon fresh cilantro leaves, snipped

2 ½ tablespoons pine nuts, toasted and crushed

Pinch of chili powder

In a large pot, caramelize the sugar over a medium heat. Remove from the heat and add the chopped onion and 2 tablespoons of water. Cook the onion over a low heat for 5 minutes.

Add the soy sauce and rice wine vinegar, then the garlic. Simmer slowly until reduced by half.

Remove from the heat and add the cilantro and pine nuts. Add a pinch of chili powder. Transfer to a glass jar with a tightly fitting lid, and use within a day or two.

Aoyama sauce

¼ cup (2 oz./50 g) sugar

Scant 1 cup (7 fl. oz./200 ml) mirin

¼ cup (2 fl. oz./60 ml) rice wine vinegar

⅓ cup (3 fl. oz./80 ml) soy sauce

1 tablespoon wasabi powder

⅓ cup (3 fl. oz./80 ml) olive oil

Juice of 1 lemon

Grated ginger root

In a large cooking pot, cook the sugar and 2 tablespoons of water to make a golden syrup. Remove from the heat and immediately add the mirin and rice vinegar to halt the coloring of the caramel. Return to the heat and stir to continue dissolving the caramel.

Remove from the heat and add the soy sauce and wasabi powder.

Mix with a stick blender to make a smooth sauce, and add the olive oil little by little.

Check the seasoning and add a little lemon juice and grated ginger to your taste.

CHEF'S NOTE I created this sauce in homage to the beautiful area of Tokyo where we opened our first restaurant in Japan. There are many beautiful buildings in this elegant area, such as the amazing Prada building designed by Swiss architects Herzog & de Meuron.

Vinegar liqueur

1 star anise

1 teaspoon ground cinnamon

1 teaspoon dried thyme leaves

1 teaspoon black peppercorns

3 ½ tablespoons sherry vinegar

Scant ½ cup (3 ½ fl. oz./100 ml) balsamic vinegar

Scant ½ cup (3 ½ fl. oz./100 ml) port

2 ½ tablespoons honey

3 ½ oz. (100 g) Muscatel grape raisins

2 ½ oz. (60 g) pear, peeled, cored, and diced

¼ cup (1 oz./30 g) dried apricots, finely diced

¼ cup (1 oz./30 g) dates, finely diced

1 piece orange peel

Wrap the star anise, cinnamon, thyme, and peppercorns in a small cheesecloth bag.

Put the sherry vinegar, balsamic vinegar, and port in a large pot. Add the honey, fruit, orange peel, and cheesecloth bag. Bring to a boil, then turn down and simmer for 1 hour. Squeeze the cheesecloth bag to extract the maximum flavor and then discard.

Transfer to a glass jar while still hot (as if you were making jam). Store in a cool place and use within 1 month.

Montpellier butter

2 oz. (50 g) shallots, finely chopped

3 ½ tablespoons cider vinegar

Scant ½ cup (3 ½ fl. oz./100 ml) dry white white

1 stick (4 oz./110 g) salted butter, softened

White pepper

Put the shallots, vinegar, and white wine in a large pot. Cook over a low heat and reduce until there is no liquid left. Season with pepper and allow to cool to room temperature.

Mix the softened butter and the cooked shallots together in a large bowl before rolling it into the desired shape. Refrigerate until needed.

Gingerbread mayonnaise

1 slice *pain d'épices*, or gingerbread

2 egg yolks

2 tablespoons mustard

Salt and freshly ground black pepper

2 cups (1 pint/500 ml) sunflower oil

Sherry vinegar

Heat the oven to 300°F/150°C/gas mark 2. Put the gingerbread in the oven to dry out, then turn it into crumbs.

Whisk the egg yolks and mustard together in a bowl and season with salt and pepper.

Add the oil little by little, a drop at a time to begin with, whisking energetically to emulsify the mayonnaise.

Finish by stirring in a dash of vinegar and the gingerbread crumbs.

Misfits relish

Olive oil, for frying

2 oz. (50 g) green bell pepper, finely chopped

Green parts of 2 scallions, chopped

Scant ½ cup (2 oz./50 g) red currants

4 teaspoons salted capers

1 tablespoon sugar

½ oz. (15 g) anchovy fillets (about 5 fillets)

¾ oz. (20 g) *soubressada* (or finely diced chorizo)

4 tablespoons sherry vinegar

2 thick slices of lemon

2 hard-boiled eggs, roughly chopped

1 tablespoon Dijon mustard

Pinch of *piment d'Espelette*, or paprika

2 tablespoons rice wine vinegar

2 cups (1 pint/500 ml) good-quality olive oil

2 tablespoons snipped chives

Table salt

Heat a little olive oil in a skillet and sauté the diced bell pepper, scallion, red currants, and capers for 3 minutes. Add the sugar and cook for a few more minutes to caramelize the sugar.

Add the anchovies and *soubressada* and cook for an additional minute. Deglaze the pan with the sherry vinegar and cook for an additional 3 minutes.

Brush the lemon slices with a little olive oil and broil for a few minutes. Cut into small dice.

Put the chopped hard-boiled eggs in the bowl of a food processor, and add the diced lemon, then the contents of the skillet. Process to mix well, then add the mustard, *piment d'Espelette*, and rice wine vinegar.

Stir in the olive oil and chives. Check the taste, and adjust to your taste—acidity, spiciness, saltiness.

Store in the fridge for up to 48 hours.

CHEF'S NOTE A reference to John Huston's *The Misfits,* Marilyn Monroe and Clark Gable's last film, this sauce is a little far-fetched—spicy, sweet, and slightly off beam.

DESERTS

Chocolate soup
with caramelized nuts

For the caramelized nuts:
2 cups (7 oz./200 g) whole skinned hazelnuts
½ cup (3 ½ oz./100 g) sugar
2 tablespoons water
Dash of hazelnut oil
Pinch of fleur de sel

For the chocolate soup:
14 oz. (400 g) dark chocolate (70 percent)
1 cup (8 ½ fl. oz./250 ml) cream
1 cup (8 ½ fl. oz./250 ml) milk

First make the caramelized nuts. Heat the oven to 300°F/150°C/gas mark 2.

Roast the hazelnuts in the oven for 15 minutes.

Meanwhile, in a cooking pot, heat the sugar and water to a temperature of 225°F (107°C). Leaving the pot on the heat, add the hazelnuts, stirring continuously, until the sugar coats the hazelnuts and they are completely caramelized. Add a dash of hazelnut oil and a pinch of fleur de sel. Pour the hazelnuts onto a cold work surface and separate them before they cool.

To make the chocolate soup, chop the chocolate and place in a heat-resistant bowl. Gently heat the cream and milk, then pour over the chopped chocolate. Mix well to make a smooth soup.

Pour a little chocolate soup into individual bowls, and scatter a few caramelized nuts over the top.

CHEF'S NOTE If you prefer, you can use almonds or pistachios instead of hazelnuts.

Chocolate tart

For the pie crust:
2 ¼ cups (8 oz./225 g) flour
⅔ cup (3 oz./90 g) confectioners' sugar
⅓ cup (1 oz./30 g) ground almonds
1 stick (4 oz./110 g) butter, diced
Pinch of salt
1 egg, beaten

For the chocolate ganache:
7 oz. (200 g) dark chocolate (70 per cent)
Scant 1 cup (7 ½ fl. oz./225 ml) cream
3 ½ tablespoons (2 oz./50 g) butter, softened

First make the pie crust. Preheat the oven to 300°F/150°C/gas mark 2.

In a large bowl, mix the flour, sugar, and ground almonds. Add the diced butter and cut in until the mixture resembles bread crumbs. Stir in the salt, then the beaten egg to bind it. Allow to rest for 30 minutes.

Roll out the dough to a thickness of ⅛–¼ in. (3–5 mm). Prick with a fork and transfer it carefully to a greased tart pan. Trim the edges and bake in the oven for 10 minutes.

To make the chocolate filling, chop the chocolate. Bring the cream to a boil in a cooking pot. Remove from the heat, add the chocolate, and mix well. Beat in the butter a little at a time to make a smooth cream. Allow to cool to room temperature.

Pour the liquid ganache into the cooked tart shell and allow to harden before serving.

Apple rice pudding
(in homage to Jean Vignard)

⅔ cup (4 oz./120 g) short-grain rice
2 cups (1 pint/500 ml) milk
⅓ cup (3 fl. oz./80 ml) light cream
⅓ cup (2 ½ oz./75 g) sugar
½ vanilla bean
1 apple (Golden Delicious)
3 ½ tablespoons lemon juice
Confectioners' sugar, to taste
Calvados, to taste

Preheat the oven to 275°F/130°C/gas mark 1.

Rinse the rice under cold water then place in a shallow ovenproof dish.

In a cooking pot, bring the milk, cream, sugar, and vanilla bean to a boil, then pour it over the rice. Cover with parchment paper, then place in the oven and cook for 1 hour.

When the rice is cooked through, remove from the oven and allow to cool for 30 minutes.

Peel and core the apple and grate it into a bowl. Sprinkle with the lemon juice, a little confectioners' sugar, and a dash of calvados.

Arrange the apples on top of the warm rice.

Heat a little more calvados, pour it over the apples, and flambé it.

CHEF'S NOTE At age fifteen, I was the last apprentice of Jean Vignard, who reigned at Chez Juliette in Lyon for twenty years. In his minuscule kitchen, this chef who had once served at the court of the king of Sweden, and who had a fondness for cravats and cigarette holders, taught me a love of detail and precision in cooking.

Fresh raspberries with Parmesan

5 basil leaves

1 lb. (500 g) fresh raspberries

2 tablespoons sugar syrup (e.g. Canadou)

5 oz. (150 g) fresh almonds

2 oz. (50 g) block Parmesan

Cut the basil leaves in half and place them in a glass bowl with the raspberries.

Pour over the sugar syrup, cover with plastic wrap, and set aside in a cool place.

Heat the broiler. Shell the almonds and remove their skins. Crush them roughly, and scatter them in the bottom of a shallow ovenproof dish. Grate the Parmesan over the almonds.

Place under the broiler for a few minutes, and broil to slightly melt the cheese.

Mix the raspberries vigorously with the syrup (for example, in a cocktail shaker), pour them over the hot almond–cheese mixture, and serve immediately, serving from the dish at the table.

CHEF'S NOTE The choice of cheese is vital in this recipe. Buy a piece of real, fresh Parmesan (if it is too old it will taste too strong).

Curried pineapple
with milk ice cream

For the milk ice cream:
2 cups (1 pint/500 ml) milk
⅔ cup (5 fl. oz./150 ml) cream
⅔ cup (4 ½ oz./130 g) sugar
¼ cup (1 ½ oz./40 g) milk powder

For the curried pineapple:
⅓ cup (2 ½ oz./75 g) sugar
1 lb. (450 g) pineapple, diced
2 pinches of Madras curry powder

Make the ice cream a day ahead. In a cooking pot, bring the milk and cream to a boil, add the sugar and milk powder, and stir together. Pour into a large bowl and set this bowl in a larger bowl filled with ice. Allow to cool, then place in an ice-cream maker and follow the manufacturer's instructions.

To make the curried pineapple, cook the sugar in a large non-stick skillet until it begins to caramelize.

Add the pineapple and curry powder and cook, stirring often, until it is caramelized.

Remove from the heat and set aside at room temperature.

To serve, place a spoonful of the curried pineapple onto each plate and top with a scoop of milk ice cream.

Mixed Drinks

Hors d'Oeuvres

Fresh Appetizers

COCKTAIL PARTY

Dips

Special Occasions

MIXED DRINKS

Green pepper cocktail

4 teaspoons green bell pepper juice
4 teaspoons pineapple juice
4 teaspoons cachaça
Pinch of snipped cilantro leaves
Crushed ice
1 lime wedge

Put the juices, cachaça, and cilantro leaves in a shaker with some crushed ice and shake.

Squeeze the lime into a martini glass and strain the shaken cocktail over the top.

Fiery Latin cocktail

2 tablespoons Campari
2 tablespoons Manzanilla (an Andalusian sherry)
2 tablespoons white port
2 tablespoons sour cherry juice
1 slice orange

Mix all the ingredients, except the orange, in a mixing glass, and pour into a tumbler. Add the orange slice.

Montreal beer

3 large raspberries

1 tablespoon maple syrup

2 tablespoons Kirsch

4 teaspoons Canadian bourbon

2 tablespoons dark beer

1 tablespoon cranberry granita

Mash the raspberries with the maple syrup in a tumbler.

Add the Kirsch, then the bourbon, and finally the dark beer. Add the cranberry granita just before serving.

Fresh tequila cocktail

A particular favorite of our photographer...

2 tablespoons tequila
2 tablespoons green apple juice
4 teaspoons cucumber juice
2 teaspoons white rum
4 mint leaves, snipped
2 arugula leaves, snipped
1 tablespoon yogurt
1 tablespoon lime granita

Put all the ingredients except the granita in a shaker and shake vigorously. Strain into a martini glass and top with the lime granita.

HORS D'OEUVRES

Couscous morsels

¼ cup (1 ¾ oz./50 g) couscous

3 ½ tablespoons vegetable stock

½ tablespoon colombo

Pinch of turmeric

Salt and freshly ground pepper

Juice of 1 lemon

2 tablespoons olive oil

1 head of lettuce

1 bunch of herbs (chervil, chives, flat-leaf parsley, etc.), chopped

Put the couscous in a bowl. Heat the vegetable stock, add the colombo, turmeric, and some pepper, and pour over the couscous. Cover with plastic wrap and allow to swell for 15 minutes.

Meanwhile, in a small bowl, mix most of the lemon juice with a pinch of salt and add the olive oil, whisking continuously.

Bring a large pot of water to a boil and blanch the whole head of lettuce for 1 minute. Remove from the boiling water and plunge it immediately into a bowl of ice water to stop the cooking process. Drain, and separate the leaves, spreading them out to dry on a wire rack.

Spread the dried lettuce leaves out on the work surface. Place a spoonful of couscous in the center of each one, sprinkle with chopped herbs, and drizzle over a little lemon dressing. Fold up the lettuce leaves to make small packages and arrange on a serving dish. Keep in the refrigerator until ready to serve.

CHEF'S NOTE Colombo is a Caribbean spice mix that includes garlic, chili, turmeric, coriander, and mustard seed.

Forbidden rice balls

Scant ½ cup (3 ½ fl. oz./100 ml) stock (made using a stock cube)

1 thyme sprig

1 bay leaf

Salt and freshly ground black pepper

½ cup (3 ½ oz./100 g) black rice (ideally Chinese black or forbidden rice)

5 oz. (150 g) cured ham, finely sliced

Pour the stock into a large pot with the thyme, bay leaf, and some salt and bring to a boil. Pour in the rice, cover, and cook for 18 minutes over a low heat until the rice has absorbed all the stock. Remove from the heat and allow to cool.

Form the cooled rice into small balls 2 in. (5 cm) in diameter, and place them on a large plate. Season with pepper and wrap each one with sliced ham. Arrange on a serving plate, cover with plastic wrap, and keep at room temperature until ready to serve.

CHEF'S NOTE For this recipe it is vital to use top-quality ham with the right proportion of melt-in-the-mouth fat. A Serrano ham would be the perfect choice.

It is preferable to use Chinese black or forbidden rice (also known as Emperor's rice) but a dark sticky rice may be substituted.

Green shiso bites

¼ cup (1 oz./25 g) Fjord® yogurt, or sour cream

Pinch of wasabi powder

½ lime

Salt and pepper

6 cooked shrimp tails

Dash of olive oil

1 ripe persimmon, chopped into large chunks

12 shiso leaves

Whisk the Fjord® with the wasabi in a small bowl. Add a few drops of lime juice and a pinch of salt.

Cut the shrimp tails in half and season with salt and a drizzle of olive oil.

Peel the persimmon and chop roughly.

Spread the shiso leaves on the work surface, squash a chunk of persimmon onto the center of each sheet, add a half shrimp tail, and top with a little Fjord sauce. Season with pepper, then fold over the leaf, and hold together with a toothpick.

Swordfish and smoked salmon bites

1 oz. (30 g) celeriac

Juice of ½ lemon

2 oz. (50 g) slice foie gras

2 sheets nori seaweed

3 slices smoked salmon

3 slices smoked swordfish

1 teaspoon wasabi

1 tablespoon roasted peanuts, finely chopped

Finely chop the celeriac, put in a bowl and sprinkle with the lemon juice. Cut the foie gras into 12 sticks. Cut the nori seaweed into 12 pieces.

Cut the slices of salmon and swordfish in half and place on the work surface. Put a dab of wasabi on each slice, then a stick of foie gras and a little celeriac. Roll up to enclose the filling and arrange on a serving plate. Sprinkle with chopped peanuts and chill until needed.

Tofu bites

2 ½ tablespoons (3 ½ oz./100 g)
   short-grain rice
1 ¾ oz. (50 g) white radish, diced
1 tablespoon snipped flat-leaf parsley

For the soy mayonnaise:
1 oz. (30 g) tofu
1 tablespoon mustard
Scant ½ cup (3 ½ fl. oz./100 ml) sunflower oil
Salt and freshly ground white pepper

In a large pot, bring 5 cups (2 ½ pints/1.2 liters) of water to a boil with a pinch of salt.

Pour in the rice, cover, and cook for 18 minutes over a low heat until all the water has been absorbed. Remove from the heat and allow to rest, keeping the pot covered.

Prepare the soy mayonnaise: in a bowl, mix the tofu with the mustard, and add the oil a little at a time. Check the seasoning. Add the diced white radish to the soy mayonnaise.

Make little balls of rice 2 in. (5 cm) in diameter. Season with pepper, then roll in the snipped parsley. Arrange on a serving plate, cover with plastic wrap and keep at room temperature until ready to serve. Serve the white rice balls with the soy mayonnaise.

Stuffed Brie de Meaux

1 Brie de Meaux
¾ oz. (20 g) truffles, chopped
Freshly ground pepper
2 tablespoons mustard
1 tablespoon white wine
½ teaspoon finely chopped lovage leaves
½ teaspoon pink peppercorns, whole
Pinch of Sichuan pepper

Cut the Brie into quarters, then slice each quarter in half horizontally.

Take the top off the first quarter, spread the chopped truffle in the middle and season with pepper. Put the top back on, and wrap in plastic wrap.

Thin the mustard with the white wine and spread this in the middle of the second quarter. Again, put the top back on, and wrap in plastic wrap.

On the third, spread the finely chopped lovage leaves, season with pepper, and wrap.

Scatter the pink peppercorns in the center of the last quarter, and season with Sichuan pepper. Wrap.

Put the four quarters together on a plate, as if the cheese were whole. Place a plate on the top as a weight, and leave for 12 hours in the refrigerator.

To serve, remove all the plastic wrap and replace the quarters on a serving plate to make a whole cheese again. Serve with toasted country-style bread and a good green salad.

CHEF'S NOTE Brie de Meaux is a soft cow's milk cheese with a white mold rind. It has a slightly bitter taste, which ripens to a sweet hazelnut aroma. You can substitute other Brie if Brie de Meaux is not available.

FRESH APPETIZERS

Endive, pear, Roquefort,
and walnuts

1 pear

Juice of ½ lemon

2 tablespoons fine sherry vinegar

3 heads of endive

2 tablespoons crème fraîche (or sour cream)

Salt and freshly ground white pepper

1 ¾ oz. (50 g) Roquefort cheese, crumbled

¼ cup (1 oz./30 g) fresh shelled walnuts (or dried chestnuts, roughly chopped)

Peel the pear and cut it into thick slices. Place on a dish, and sprinkle with a little lemon juice and sherry vinegar.

Remove about a dozen whole endive leaves and set aside to use as scoops. Finely chop the remaining leaves, discarding the bitter heart.

In a bowl, mix the crème fraîche with the remaining sherry vinegar and a few drops of lemon juice. Season with salt and add the chopped endives, crumbled Roquefort, and chopped walnuts.

Fill the endive leaves with this mixture and top each with a slice of pear.

Place in the refrigerator for a few minutes before serving. Season with pepper just before serving.

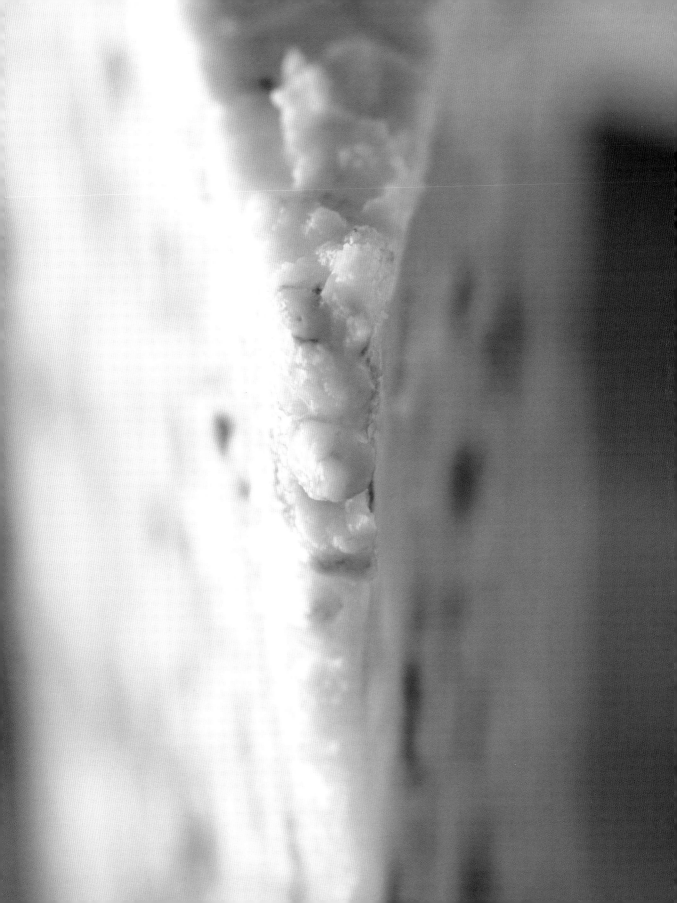

Florets of cauliflower
and Romanesco with pineapple and broccoli tips

10 ½ oz. (300 g) cauliflower
10 ½ oz. (300 g) Romanesco broccoli
1 head of broccoli
½ Victoria pineapple
2 tablespoons grained mustard
2 tablespoons organic hazelnut oil
Pinch of salt

Bring a large pot of boiling water to a boil. Snap the cauliflower and the Romanesco broccoli into evenly sized florets. Cook in boiling water for 5 minutes until al dente. Remove with a slotted spoon and immediately drop them into a bowl of ice water, then drain.

Using a sharp knife, trim the broccoli florets, removing the stem to leave just the tips. Place them in a fine metal sieve or basket and plunge them in the boiling water for 2 minutes. Remove and refresh in ice water, then drain.

Finely dice the pineapple, reserving the juice. Mix the juice with the mustard, and add the hazelnut oil and a pinch of salt.

Arrange the cauliflower and Romanesco florets in a serving dish, scatter over the pineapple cubes, pour over the mustard sauce, and sprinkle with the tips of broccoli. Serve chilled.

Sweet-and-sour cherry tomatoes
with smoked duck and snails

18 cherry tomatoes on the vine

2 tablespoons olive oil

Salt and freshly ground black pepper

2 tablespoons maple syrup

1 smoked duck breast

2 dozen snails (*petit-gris, Helix aspersa*)

1 tablespoon sherry vinegar

4 green basil leaves, snipped

Using scissors, snip the cherry tomatoes off the vine, leaving the stalk.

Heat the oil in a skillet, add the tomatoes, and season. Cook for 45 minutes over a low heat, then add the maple syrup. Continue to cook, stirring regularly, until the tomatoes are softened and burst. Finely chop the smoked duck breast and add to the skillet along with the snails.

Turn carefully to combine, then sprinkle with the vinegar and scatter over the basil. Just before serving, season generously with pepper and serve in the skillet.

Curried mushroom pâté
with pastry puffs

14 oz. (400 g) firm white button mushrooms

1 ½ tablespoons (¾ oz./20 g) butter

1 shallot, finely chopped

Table salt

¼ teaspoon curry powder

¼ teaspoon paprika

Scant ½ cup (3 ½ fl. oz./100 ml) light cream

1 slice ham, cut into ⅛ in. (3 mm) dice

20 mini pastry puffs, or crackers

Using a mandoline, cut 12 fine slices of mushroom, and set aside on a plate covered with plastic wrap. Chop the remaining mushrooms roughly.

Heat the butter in a skillet and sweat the shallot, without coloring. When they are transparent, add the chopped mushrooms. Salt lightly, cover with a lid, and cook for 5 minutes over a low heat until the mushrooms give off their water. Remove the lid, and cook for an additional 5 minutes, still over a low heat.

When the mushroom liquid has cooked off (and the mushrooms have been cooked into what is known as a "duxelles"), add the curry powder and paprika, then the cream. Cook for an additional 5 minutes. Check the seasoning, and add the diced ham. Cover with plastic wrap and set aside at room temperature.

Serve the mushroom pâté in a bowl, with the sliced mushrooms arranged on top. Serve with warm pastry puffs.

DIPS

Lime-flavored avocado
with mango and mustard sauce

1 very ripe yellow mango
Scant ½ cup (3 ½ fl. oz./100 ml) condensed milk
1 tablespoon mustard powder (e.g. Colman's)
Salt
1 large avocado
Juice of 1 lime
Pinch of chili powder

Peel the mango, remove the pit, and cut the flesh into large cubes. Process the mango flesh to make a thick purée. Mix in the condensed milk and the mustard powder. Season lightly with salt.

Cut the avocado in half, remove the pit, and cut the flesh into large cubes. Arrange the cubes in a shallow dish, sprinkle with lime juice, and season lightly with salt.

Pour the mango sauce over the avocados and sprinkle with a little chili powder. Cover with plastic wrap and place in the refrigerator for 10 minute.

Serve chilled, for example with shreds of grilled chicken.

Potato and haddock purée
with a hint of juniper

3 large potatoes (Bintje, for example, or other good mashing potato)

7 oz. (200 g) haddock fillet

Milk

Salt and freshly ground black pepper

Scant ½ cup (3 ½ fl. oz./100 ml) horseradish cream

Scant ½ cup (3 ½ fl. oz./100 ml) olive oil

Zest of 1 organic lemon

3 ½ tablespoons juniper liqueur (e.g. Houlle)

6 thin green cabbage leaves

Cook the potatoes in their skins in a large pot of boiling, salted water until cooked through (this could take about 30 minutes or more for large potatoes). Meanwhile, put the haddock in a skillet, cover with milk, add salt and pepper, and bring to a simmer. Remove from the heat and leave for 5 minutes to poach in the milk. Remove from the pan and allow to cool on a plate.

Drain the cooked potatoes, remove the skin, and mash. Add the horseradish cream, little by little, then the olive oil, beating all the while with a wooden spoon. Continue beating the mashed potato, adding the lemon zest, seasoning, and juniper liqueur.

Flake the cooked haddock, and cut the cabbage leaves into large squares.

Serve the mashed potatoes, cabbage leaves, and haddock in separate bowls.

Allow guests to serve themselves—take a cabbage leaf and place a spoonful of mashed potato and a little haddock in the center, roll up … and enjoy!

Tandoori white beans with gin

7 oz. (200 g) very large white beans (e.g. Tarbais)

1 bouquet garni

1 onion, studded with cloves

Salt and pepper

For the marinade:

4 tablespoons olive oil

1 tablespoon tomato paste

1 tablespoon sweet paprika

½ tablespoon tandoori spices

2 tablespoons gin

A day ahead, soak the dried beans in cold water.

The following day, drain the beans and place them in a pressure cooker. Cover with cold water and add the bouquet garni, clove-studded onion, and a pinch of salt. Close and cook in the pressure cooker for 20 minutes.

Meanwhile, prepare the marinade. Heat the olive oil in a skillet and cook the tomato paste. Add the spices and cook for an additional 5 minutes over a low heat. Thin out the sauce a little with the gin and allow to cool.

Drain the beans, add them to the sauce and stir carefully to coat. Check the seasoning and season with salt if necessary. Cover with plastic wrap and place in the refrigerator for several hours. Stir again before serving, and serve in small dishes with teaspoons.

CHEF'S NOTE Tarbais beans are a gourmet white bean grown in southwestern France, near the Spanish border. They are prized for their thin skin and non-floury texture.

Fava bean hummus
with ham-wrapped breadsticks

7 oz. (200 g) frozen fava beans, peeled
Scant 1 cup (7 fl. oz./200 ml) olive oil
Juice of 1 lemon
1 garlic clove, crushed
1 teaspoon ground cumin
Salt and freshly ground white pepper
12 thin slices of prosciutto, sliced into strips
12 breadsticks

Bring a large pot of salted water to a boil and cook the fava beans for 10 minutes until you can squash them easily between finger and thumb. Drain, reserving a little of the cooking liquid, and refresh under cold running water.

Place in the bowl of a food processor and process to a purée. Add the olive oil a little at a time, then the lemon juice, garlic, and cumin. If necessary, thin out the purée with a little of the cooking liquid. Check the seasoning. Scrape into a bowl, cover with plastic wrap and store in the refrigerator.

Roll the ham round the breadsticks.

Serve the fava bean hummus in small bowls with the ham-wrapped breadsticks. You can add slices of pita bread, too, if needed.

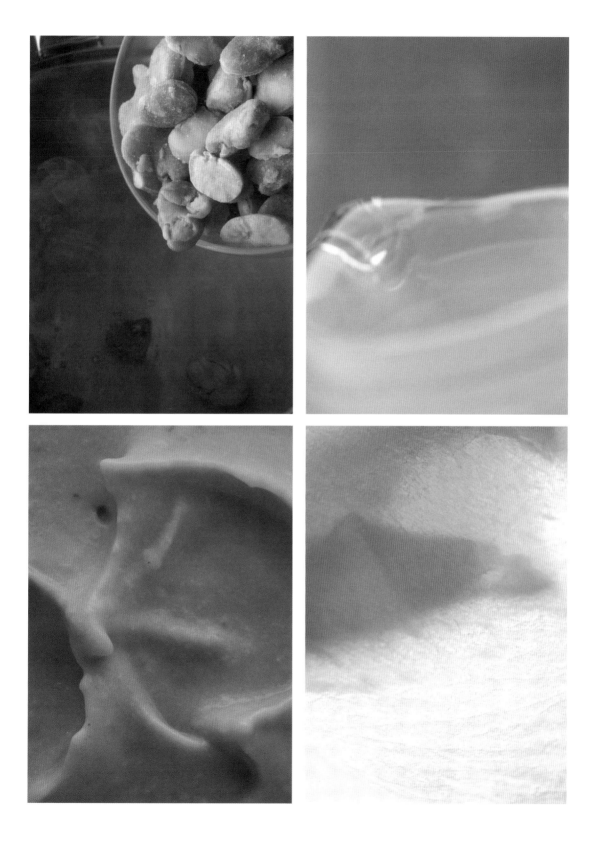

Eggplant, olive, and onion confit dip
with melon, watermelon, and pear

2 eggplants

2 ½ cups (1 pint/600 ml) mineral water

½ cup (4 fl. oz./120 ml) rice wine vinegar

1 small onion, finely chopped

2 tablespoons olive oil

1 cardamom pod, crushed

2 tablespoons tahini

Salt and freshly ground white pepper

¼ watermelon, cubed

½ lemon, peeled and segmented

10 green olives, pitted and finely chopped

1 tablespoon toasted sesame seeds

1 melon, cubed

1 slightly underripe pear, sliced

Preheat the oven to 325°F/160°C/gas mark 3.

Put the whole eggplants in the oven, and cook for 20–25 minutes, until the skin is loose and the flesh soft.

Meanwhile, heat the water with the rice wine vinegar in a large pot and briefly blanch the onion. Drain, reserving the cooking liquid.

Heat the oil in a large pot, then add the cardamom pod and blanched onion. Season with salt and pepper, and allow to cook for 20 minutes over a low heat.

When the eggplants are cooked, remove from the oven, cut in half, and scoop out the flesh with a spoon. Process the flesh in the bowl of a food processor with the tahini.

Add the eggplant purée to the pot, stir, and check the seasoning.

Place the watermelon cubes and lemon segments in the cooled cooking liquid from the onions. Allow to infuse for 15 minutes.

Stir the chopped olives into the eggplant purée and sprinkle with the sesame seeds. Serve in separate bowls the eggplant purée, melon cubes, pear slices, and marinated watermelon.

Serve with cubes of foie gras or deli meats.

Watercress purée
with merguez sausages

3 large potatoes (Bintje, for example)
7 oz. (200 g) watercress, stems removed
Scant ½ cup (3 ½ fl. oz./100 ml) olive oil
3 merguez sausages
Salt and pepper

Cook the potatoes, whole and unpeeled, in a large pot of boiling salted water.

Meanwhile, pour 1 cup of water into a cooking pot and bring to a boil. Add the watercress with a pinch of salt and a drop of olive oil and cook for 5–7 minutes until the stalks are cooked through. Drain, reserving the cooking liquid. Process in a food processor, adding cooking liquid if necessary to make a thick purée.

Grill the merguez, and cut into small pieces. Keep warm.

Drain the potatoes, remove the skins, and mash to make a smooth purée. Add the watercress purée little by little, then the olive oil, beating continuously with a wooden spoon. Check the seasoning.

Serve the watercress purée with the merguez on the side.

Cantal entre-deux
with fresh cream cheese

¾ cup (5 oz./150 g) fresh *faisselle* cream cheese, such as Sarasson or Quark

2 tablespoons vinegar

2 tablespoons walnut oil

1 shallot, finely chopped

1 small bunch of chives, snipped

1 tarragon sprig, snipped

Salt and freshly ground pepper

7 oz. (200 g) Cantal entre-deux cheese

Slices of baguette, toasted

Combine the fresh cream cheese with the vinegar and walnut oil. Add the shallot, chives, and tarragon and season with salt and pepper. Transfer to a small bowl and place in the refrigerator.

Cut the Cantal cheese into thin slices.

Serve the bowl of soft cheese with the slices of Cantal and slices of toasted baguette.

CHEF'S NOTE Sarasson is a fresh cream cheese produced in Saint-Etienne and in the Loire Valley. It is produced from buttermilk dropped into boiling water. The small grains of cheese rise to the surface, then are drained and formed into larger balls. It is generally seasoned with herbs—chives, garlic, salt, and pepper, and is often eaten with steamed or boiled potatoes. You can substitute any fresh cow's milk cheese, such as Quark.

Cantal entre-deux cheese is a medium-aged cow's milk cheese that is firm and ivory-colored. Substitute a medium Cheddar if it is not available.

Red onion and blood sausage purée
with star anise

4 large red onions

1 ½ tablespoons (¾ oz./20 g) butter

1 star anise

Pinch of brown sugar

7 oz. (200 g) blood sausage

Salt and pepper

1 cooked beet, cut into large chunks

1 bunch of small radishes, trimmed and washed

Peel the red onions and cut them into quarters. Place them in a large cooking pot with the butter, a scant cup (7 fl. oz./200 ml) water, the star anise, and the sugar. Cover and cook for 30 minutes over a low heat, stewing them in the liquid. You may have to add a little more water during the cooking time.

When the onions are ready—they should be very soft, so that you can squash them with a spoon—remove from the heat, take out the star anise, and drain the onions, returning the cooking liquid to the pot.

Place the blood sausage in the pot and heat through in the onion cooking liquid. Remove from the pot and remove skin.

Process the cooked onions, adding the skinless blood sausage a little at a time. Add a little butter to taste.

Serve the purée hot in a bowl with the beet and radishes on the side.

SPECIAL OCCASIONS

PREPARATION TIME: 10 MINUTES • FREEZING TIME: 2 HOURS • SERVES 2

A dozen oysters, Riesling granita,
and fresh cilantro

½ bottle Riesling

Bunch of fresh cilantro (leaves only)

12 oysters

Crushed ice

Pour the Riesling into a shallow dish and place it in the freezer. Freeze for several hours, scratching regularly with a fork until it forms a granita. Snip the cilantro. Open the oysters and keep in a cool place. Place the granita in a bowl set over a larger bowl filled with crushed ice. Eat the oysters, adding a spoonful of granita to each one, sprinkled with cilantro.

PREPARATION TIME: 15 MINUTES • COOKING TIME: 10 MINUTES • SERVES 2

Onion soup

Scant 1 cup (7 fl. oz./200 ml) full-fat cream

8 tablespoons port

2 tablespoons (1 oz./25 g) butter

2 sweet onions, finely chopped

Pinch of sugar

Bottle of champagne

½ stock cube

Salt and freshly ground black pepper

2 oz. (50 g) Gruyère cheese, grated

Whip the cream and mix in the port. Set the whipped cream aside in the refrigerator. Melt the butter in a large cooking pot and sweat the onions until soft. Add the sugar and allow to caramelize for 5 minutes. Pour in 3 tablespoons of champagne and bring to a boil. Crumble in the stock cube, season generously with pepper, and cook for 5 minutes (while you finish off the rest of the bottle of champagne!). Pour the onion soup into two warmed bowls and sprinkle with the Gruyère cheese. Add a generous spoonful of the port-flavored cream to each bowl and serve immediately.

Index